LETTERS TO MY PEOPLE

Thoughts of a Recovering Addict

ANTHONY TORRES

Letters To My People
Copyright © 2021 by Anthony Torres

Paperback ISBN: 978-0-578-89758-5
Hardcover ISBN: 978-0-578-9008-7

This book is dedicated to **Ray Montoya-Foltz**

"I'm FREE. You can't hurt me no more.
As sad as I was to leave, I'm FREE. You can't hurt me no more
As painful as life got, I'm FREE. You can't hurt me no more
As much as I loved to smile, I'm FREE. You can't hurt me no more
As much as I loved to laugh, I'm FREE. You can't hurt me no more
As much as I loved to be with my family, I'm FREE. You can't hurt me no more"

I'm free, and you can't hurt me no more. It may look like you won, but I am alive more than ever. I am free more than ever. You have no more grip on my life. I will wait here for my family. I am in a place of no more pain, no more tears, no more addiction! You can't hurt me no more, AND I AM FREE!

ACKNOWLEDGMENTS

To my kids, Angelina, Bella, Iliana and Caleb; I love you so much.

A lot of time and tears went into writing this book. Thanks to you guys for letting me share it with the world. Thank you for the support and love you have for me. I hope you all are proud to have a dad like me, and always remember that it's not how we start life, but how we finish.

To my Queen (wife), I love you! Thank you for never giving up on us and letting me pour every bit of energy I have into writing this and making it a reality. I'm quite sure I couldn't have done this without your blessing and support. I really appreciate that.

Love and blessings,
Anthony Torres

"You won't find another book quite like my friend Anthony Torres' debut *Letters to My People: Thoughts of a Recovering Addict*.

These very personal experiences that Anthony shares in letter form have a unique way of taking you into the consciousness of someone so lost in the black hole of their drug induced reality that it would appear impossible for them to escape.

There is an enormous dose of hope found in *Letters to My People*, and I believe, without a doubt, that this book is going to be a breeding ground for miracles.

The world doesn't need anymore watered down, weak self-help books! The world needs true, genuine, down and dirty life stories like Anthony's that don't sugar coat, but give the raw authentic, "tell it like it is" truth!"

— **Brian "Head" Welch**
Co-founder of the Grammy Award winning band Korn, New York Times best-selling author of Save Me From Myself, and the subject of the Showtime documentary Loud Krazy Love.

FOREWORD

In 2009, I had just gotten out of rehab after being in there for only 12 days, and I realized I was back to being addicted to cocaine, pills, and sometimes, meth. I was also a chronic alcoholic and abused my body and mind for almost 12 years. Suicide, depression had gotten the best of me, and I wanted to end my life.

Fortunately, I was saved in a small church in Altus, Oklahoma, "Healing Waters," and gave my life to Christ.

I had been addicted for so long, and this new life was something new to me.

With a computer in front of me and Wintergreen's skoal in my bottom lip, I began to write my thoughts and life. These are my writings; this is ten years in the making.

Over the years, I have written more materials, and over time, I combined everything I had to let you know my thoughts and share what addiction felt like in my life. Suppose I had to write letters to those suffering from addictions, it would be titled, "Letters to my people."

TABLE OF CONTENTS

"We all want a great outcome, but we NEVER want to go through the process of getting there."

LETTER 1

THOUGHTS ABOUT
'WHEN I GROW UP'

D o you remember your elementary school days when
your teacher asked a question like, "What do you
want to be when you grow up?" And those hands ea-
gerly went up, with students saying, "I want to be a fireman"
"I want to be a painter," and so on.

Many kids also wanted to be what their parents were, and
it was in this moment you thought of the 'Kindergarten Cop'
movie when Arnold Schwarzenegger asked the kids, "Who is
your daddy, and what does he do?" And we heard answers
like, "I want to be like my dad. He is a policeman," or "I want
to be like my mom. She is a nurse at the hospital."

But not once in the history of teachers asking that question
did anyone say, "When I grow up, I want to be like my mom;
she's always strung out on drugs," or "When I grow up, I want
to be an alcoholic and go through two marriages." I don't think
you've ever heard any kid say, "When I grow up, I want to
overdose twice and push away everyone that I love," or "When
I grow up, I want to be a stripper hooked on cocaine,
letting countless men touch my body." I'm also very sure you
haven't

heard a kid say, "When I grow up, I want to be a prostitute and sleep with different men every 20 mins. I want to give my body away," "When I grow up, I want to wreck my life and be so heavily addicted to pills," or "When I grow up, I want to die at a very young age due to a DWI."

We never heard these words from kids. WHY? This is because our hearts were so pure and innocent then. So what changed? Was it life? Was it our past? Was it the pain caused by others? Was it the behaviors we saw our parents addicted to? Was it something that just started out so innocent; something social that we now found our lives spiraling out of control due to addictions? Was it the prescription pills we took after surgery, and now we can't stop taking them?

Here is a thought; you're no longer a little kid. You have now grown up and found yourself in this place of addiction. A place you thought you would never be. We need to be careful with saying, "Being addicted can never happen to me, or it's just a thing for the weak." The truth is, it can happen to anyone that flirts with substance abuse or anything that alters our chemical imbalance. But guess what? I don't care how far you think you are gone or how out of reach you are. Your story doesn't have to end in your addiction.

Hi, my name is Anthony, and I have four kids and a beautiful wife I so much adore. I also pastor a church in Alamogordo, NM called Mountain View Church. And yes, I believe in Jesus Christ. Don't worry! I won't get all preachy on you, I promise. This book is not aimed at pressing my beliefs on you but simply sharing my life, battles, seasons of darkness, regrets, and tears with you. I am ashamed of the things I had done, but the spotlight is not on me. The content of this book is about you being a better person. It's about you winning this war against addictions! In this book, I will be so personal with you that it will be raw and real. And as a result, when you're done reading, you will be able to say, "If he could get through it, so can I." "If he can continue to fight, so can I."

People may see me now and think, *WOW! He has a really good life.* I will say, even to this day, I have had struggles with my health and even my children's health and emotional state. We have gone through battles as a family and even seasons of difficult times. I would say, "Yes, I am blessed," but I can tell you something. To this point, people have no idea what we have been through as a family; all the lost times, tears, lost years with my kids, many wounds and scars. Addiction doesn't just affect one person; it affects everyone. Your spouse, kids, parents, everyone close to you. And somewhere in our lives, we have to see how it affects everything around us. It took me almost nine years to see what I was doing. I don't want that for you.

You should know I now live a clean and sober life. I no longer turn to alcohol or drugs to cope with life or even to be social with people. I find other healthy avenues for being social and coping with whatever life brings. Addict or not, life comes at us from all different angles, and we go through all different seasons in life. I think my only addiction, if we even want to call it that, is COFFEE. I hate to say it, but I have become a coffee snob over the years.

I am not sure how you got this book, but let me say I am really glad you are reading it. I want to make it an easy read for you and make it to the point that you can reflect and begin to process your thoughts in your own life when you're done reading.

This book actually began ten years ago, and it started with snuff in my mouth and a heart full of thoughts. Over the years, I had several written, went back to the drawing board, wrote again, and now here we are. It's also been ten years and six months since I have been clean and sober. And the truth is, I give Christ all the glory because I couldn't have done it without Him. Are you still there? Great! For some reason, someone mentions Jesus, and everyone loses their mind.

Hey! I get it! Trust me, I hated and kept my distance from people who called themselves Christians for a very long time. I even hated God for years!

But here we are, together on this journey. Whether you're a Christian or not, you're also on this journey called life. Before I end, let me just say this. You may not see a way out of your circumstances, and you may not see a new life or a life of being clean and sober. You may feel like your life is always going to be this way. It's not! You might feel like you will never make amends with your children or never restore your marriage. You will make it, and you will surely overcome this. But chew on this thought for a second. We all want a great outcome, but we NEVER want to go through the process of getting there. This will be a process only you can finish; it won't be handed to you. You have to put in work; every day! Sadly, some people don't get to live a sober and clean life because they fail to put in work. Listen, friend. You have to work, and it will surely pay off. I believe you have that drive and energy in you, and hopefully, you will realize that after reading this book.

Remember what I said regarding people's views about my life, but they failed to see what I have been through. They didn't see the process it took to get here. Everything always looks good on the outside of everyone's life, but when you start peeling back the layers of their life, you begin to see pain, scars, and times of hardship.

I wouldn't change the process for anything, no matter how hard it got. This is because it made me who I am today and made my family believe in who they are today.

So are you ready? Are you ready for me to share my thoughts and life with you? Are you ready to read about my battles and even my family's struggles? Are you ready to do some real soul searching in your own life? Are you ready to see your life for whatever it is and what it can become? Not this life of addiction, but a life of being sober and clean. That's what I want for you, friend, and that is the whole purpose of writing this book. I really pray this book speaks to someone. In life, reading books like this is the easy part, but applying things I talk about is the challenging part.

Thank you for reading this book, and I hope it blesses you and speaks to the depths of your soul in a great way. I also hope it touches you, regardless of what corner of the world you are.

If you're reading this book from the jail, prison, rehab, or know anyone who needs to read it, don't hesitate to pass it on to the next brother or sister dealing with addictions. I get you! You're my people. I have been where you are. Enjoy "Letters to my People"

Much love,
Anthony Torres

You think there is nothing worth

saving, but you're mistaken.

LETTER 2

THOUGHTS ABOUT
'HOW WILL IT END FOR YOU? HOW WILL YOU DIE?'

The numbers of addiction are staggering and growing at an alarming rate. In the United States, about 130 people die daily from an overdose. As I type this, someone just died; a mother and father just lost a son and daughter on life support due to an OD. As I type this, someone's life is getting turned upside down due to addictions. Kids are away from parents, and parents are away from their kids due to death or jail. I really am not sure how I survived those years of being addicted to cocaine, popping pills, and being an alcoholic. I tried heroin a few times, but it just was not for me. The problem was that I was a functioning addict, and those are the worst ones because they don't see they need help or see a problem with their addiction. We will talk more about it in the next thought.

We all have to die, but we just don't know when. Monthly, I sit with countless men and women in meetings to show them what it looks like to live a clean and sober life. In our addiction class, "New Life," we teach people what it looks like to continue to be clear-headed and clean with our faith-based program.

If there ever is a time my heart completely breaks, it is when I sit with someone in my office or meet someone in our group meetings and later hear they passed due to an overdose. I could see they were so close to breaking that addiction, so close to having a life of being clean and sober, and so close to having a normal healthy life without drugs and alcohol. I don't see their smiles anymore. I don't get to hear the voices of them sharing their struggles or good times.

What happened? They gave in to the pressures of life and probably said, "This will be the last time I do this." Unknowingly, it was the last time they would take a breath on this earth because they already had too much and overdosed.

One time, I met with this gentleman in my office, and he struggled and battled. I prayed with him, loved him, and told him he could win this battle. I then gave him a plan to follow; things he needed to work on. As time went by, he didn't stick to the process, and alcohol killed him. When I heard the news of his passing, I was devastated, and I cried.

The same thing happened when I heard of a young girl who attended our "New Life" class. She overdosed, died, and left two kids behind. Doing any program or rehab is not an easy fix. It takes time and dedication to get to a place of being sober and clean, but it can be done.

Hearing these stories never made it easy for me; it's a wound that heals and then reopens again. I think the ones that really got to me are those involving men who come to the church, and I see them every Sunday. I have great conversations with them, and one day, I stop seeing them. I keep in touch the best way I can, but we lose touch with each other for whatever reason. Then I bump into their loved ones at the grocery store and say, "How is Mr. X doing?" And they reply," Oh! You didn't hear. He passed away from an overdose a few months ago," and then they add, "Thank you for trying to help them in their time of need."

To this day, I take stories like that really hard. So hard that I sometimes grieve all day because I always ask myself if I could have done more. It's really heartbreaking to see a mother and father hover over their child hooked up to a ventilator machine. They hug and kiss the child as tears run down their faces, knowing that this will be the last time they'll see the child; no more conversations, laughter, or smiles. Over to me, praying over the dying child as the machine makes a beeping noise in the background, and then the doctor comes in to take the child off the machine. I see a son, daughter, father, or mother taking their last breath on earth, and I see how addiction got the best of them. I see that pain for what it really is for that family.

Countless men and women are never getting their liver transplants due to cirrhosis of the liver. Personally, I have seen so many deaths and tears to last me for life.

Going back to our old ways is a journey that can be hard. It is a journey that we war with sometimes. But before I go to my next thought, could you do me a favor? Go get a pencil. Go, I will wait.

Now turn the page; it will be blank.

I want you to go to the top of the page and write, "How will it end for me?"

The blank piece of paper is the NEW life you will have. Listen, your past won't define who you are, and it is a place I never want you to go back to. I want you to move forward; new goals, new visions, and new YOU!

I asked you how it will end for you, and this is the reason – what will kill you? Your addiction or life?

When I counsel people, I tell them their addiction will be the end of them if they don't stop. I have become so bold over the years when I counsel people. You are alive today to make that change. You are alive today to take those steps in getting your kids back. You are alive today to work on things you have been neglecting. It is time to show people you can do this, but most importantly, it's time to show yourself.

On that blank piece of paper, I want you to write your goals. When you wake up every morning, you should aim towards achieving those goals. Those GOALS that keep you driven! The goals that keep you moving forward! They're the goals that keep you going.

If you are reading this and are in detox, please finish it out. And if you are getting ready to go to a program, do your best to finish it. Do not substitute your detox for a long-term rehab program, and just get out and think that is it. There is always more in the life of recovery. Even today, I am still working on myself daily to ensure I never go back to my old ways.

In my opinion, it took you years to get to this point. Those demons are real, and I do hope you can overcome them. Okay, let me back up. YOU CAN OVERCOME THEM! If I had known about these great, faith-based, long-term programs or any program period, I might have attended, but my story is slightly different. I know you are reading this and thinking there is no more good in you. You think there is nothing worth saving, but you're mistaken. You can get back what you have lost! I am your biggest fan! And I am cheering you on because I believe in you! I also want you to believe in yourself again. Get ready! We have a lot of work to do. Let's put our fighting gloves on and start fighting back!

Much love,
Anthony Torres

"Little you, you WILL MAKE
IT!"

LETTER 3

THOUGHTS ABOUT
'HEY, LITTLE YOU!'

Hey, little you! I bet you are wondering what turn your life will take. Who will you marry? How many kids will you have? What job will you have? Right now, you have a He-Man and a Lion-O from Thundercat in your hand. Every day, you play with your friend down the street. You love eating Cheetos, knowing that they will get stuck in your teeth, and you're okay with yellow teeth for a while. You also enjoy the coconut snow-cones that turn your tongue blue.

Your mom was 16 when she had you, and her life has completely changed. Her high school days were cut short, and she now takes care of you. Your dad works hard, and you have grandparents who adore you and spoil you rotten. *What Mijo wants, Mijo gets!* Dunkin Donut munchkins were always a treat. I mean, you are the first grandkid in the Rodriquez family, and you have no worries in the world. Life is good for you!

But little you, things will change very quickly, and it will hurt you. Your grandparents will die together; a drunk driver will kill them. You will be confused and won't understand what is going on. You will just know that they aren't coming back anymore. I am sorry, no more rides in Grandpa's truck, no more toy trips, or Dunkin donut trips.

Little you, your parents will divorce. You will think that it's your fault, but it isn't. Things just happen. Your little life will be altered. If you weren't already confused, you are now. You will deal with rejection, and you will struggle with low self-esteem. You will feel like you have to pick a side every year with your parents because they are at war, always fighting with each other. But know that they both love you! Again, I am sorry this happened. You are still healing from losing your grandparents.

Little you, you will be molested and hurt. You will be touched. They don't care if you told them to stop or not. There will be no sense in telling people what went wrong because no one will believe you.

Little you, you will hear words like, "You're worthless," "You're a coward," "You're a deadbeat dad," "You will become a nobody," "You're a loser."

Little you, you will try your best to fit in, but you will always be looked down on. You will think you're a gangster, and you'll fight. You will fight because you're angry and don't know why. You will get stabbed in your hand, be shot at once, beaten up, and hated for just being you. You will have a hard time finding who you are and even fit in with others. You will always be the outcast

Little you, you will let your addiction control you. You will hurt your kids, loved ones and push everyone you know away. You will be your own worst enemy.

Little you, you will grow up and not be smart. People will make fun of you because they know you're not smart. You will become addicted to cocaine, pills, ice, and you will be an alcoholic. You will deal with depression, suicide, and anxiety. You will open up doors you wish you never opened.

Little you, there will be a time you will put a gun to your head with your hand shaking so bad, and you will feel your finger slowly going back and forth on the trigger. And all you can think of while tears run down the side of your face and boogers bubble out of your nose is, "Life would be better without me. That way, I can't hurt anyone anymore." You really don't want to die; you really just want the voices and pain to stop.

Little you, you will deal with discouragement and spiritual heaviness to the point of it keeping you up at night. Sleepless nights will happen, and your days will be tiring.

Little you, you will have a hard time looking at yourself in the mirror because you are disgusted with the man you have become.

Little you, people will laugh at you, mock you, and belittle you.

Little you, I wish I could tell you that the devil will stop chasing you, but he won't. He doesn't disappear once we grow up.

Little you, sometimes, depression will get the best of you! It will twist you, hurt you, make you feel like there is a weight on the tips of your shoulder blades, but you will have brighter days. The depression won't keep you down for long. Trust me; there is nothing wrong with you. Press through, little one!

Little you, your demons will visit you in your dreams. What doors did you open?

Little you, I know some things about the future that will hurt you, damage you, break you and make you feel down. People and the world will kick you while you are down. Just cover your face and take the blows.

Little you, I need you to hear this! Things will get better; you need to hang on. Don't give up. Believe me when I say it will get so hard for you, and sometimes, you will be lost. You will have to dig deep in your own emotions, but there will be better days ahead of you.

If you knew how much you would go through in life, would you still be in a hurry to grow up?

Little you, you will be an OVERCOMER!
Little you, you will be the ODDS!
Little you, you will be somebody!
Little you, you will be an overachiever!
Little you, you will be happy!
Little you, you WILL MAKE IT!

Much love,
Older you

The problem wasn't that I was an addict; the real problem was that I was a functioning one.

LETTER 4

THOUGHTS ABOUT
'AM I REALLY AN ADDICT?'

If anyone ever asks me if I had any regrets in life, it would be many things. Drugs made me lose quality time with my kids. If you want to be a better person than I am, try to get help sooner. I can never get back those lost times, even till today. Sometimes it's like a movie that keeps playing in my head, although it has gotten better over the years

The problem wasn't that I was an addict; the real problem was that I was a functioning one. To me, those are the worst kind of addicts. That denial, pride, and ego run deep in our hearts. What we see as functioning, others see it as us being blind to our problems. Those struggling with addiction say, "Well, I pay the bills," "I still go to work and provide for my family," "I don't really have a problem." I can't tell you how many times I laid on the cold cement floor in the restroom, resting my head at work because I had been up for days.

I was throwing up everything I had in my stomach, just trying to make it through the day, with my head throbbing and popping aspirin to make it stop. I can't mention how many times I would sneak a quick bump (cocaine) chopped up on the toilet sink just so I can get a burst of high for the day. And the sad part was that I would go back out to drink after work.

We have all said this same line before, "I don't need any help, and I can do this on my own," or "I don't need to speak to any Counselor." You then blink, and years have gone by; you've lost times with your kids; you've had multiple fights with your spouse to the point that some had ended in domestic violence and probably landed you in jail or divorce; you've lost multiple jobs because you didn't make it to work; lost friendships, careers, and dreams. These are lost times we can never get back. Time is precious and valuable. Things get bad in our lives, and we ask ourselves, "Am I really an addict?" Again, I truly believe that functioning addicts are their own worst enemy because they assume everyone else has the problem. They assume everyone else is complaining, but they fail to see their problems and the causes. They fail to see the root of things. Listen, every bad thing in life has an origin. For me, it was my addiction! Again, ask yourself, "Am I really an addict?"

One crisp, cool night, I had been drinking in my garage, washing my motorcycle, and listening to *Journey* as I was having a few beers. I was already as high as a building in New York. Iliana was riding her bike in the driveway as I viewed the sunset of New Mexico's sky. I had just finished my stash of coke from the other night, and I needed more. I told myself that I didn't need more and did my best to keep it together. I could see things play out in my mind if I left, but I was slowly giving in. That temptation was already planted, and it just continued to grow. It was too much for me now, and I knew my high was about to come down. My body had already had an intolerance for more drugs.

I hear people say things like, "How could my husband/wife/child act the way they do? Can't they just stop?" No! That's why they are called addicts. They need more of that same feeling; that high. We don't want to come down, and we will do what we can to keep back up. That's why we lie, steal, betray, and hurt people we love. We love the high more than our current state. Sadly, we love the high more than our family, even more than life itself. I don't think we really want to hurt anyone; it's just that sensation of the high we want to feel.

If there was one thing Sasha (my wife) was really good at, it was sensing when I was about to get an itch to leave to get more drugs. She already knew what I was doing. She learned to study my body language and speech. All she ever wanted was peace —peace in our home, lives, and hearts. Sadly, with addiction there is never peace, only war! With her gentle voice, she would try to talk me out of it. Not talking down to me, but somehow trying to get me not to go. And I always respected her for that. She would say, "Let's have a family night? I will cook, and we can watch movies and cuddle." She knew what she was doing. She was doing her best to defuse any situation, and she really did her best. But the voices of addiction just got louder over the years, and her sweet voice was neutralized. Over the months and now turning into years, my addiction had overshadowed my love for Sasha and my family. Drugs had a strong hold on me, and my family was no match for that.

When she saw that she was losing control of me, and nothing was working, she fought for me to stay, and she fought hard. She did this because she knew I would damage and abuse my body. She tried to stop me from destroying my mind, darkening my heart, and ripping apart everything we had worked so hard for as a family. She was trying to save me from myself, and sadly, I just saw her as my enemy every time. And I had no choice but to fight back; my addiction had a bulldog grip on me.

At this point, nothing was working. So Sasha decided to jump on my bike seat and said, "You're not going anywhere." With drunken rage and anger in my eyes, I said, "Please leave me alone. Let me leave. I will be right back." With concern on her face at this point, she said, "No! I know where you are going." And I replied, "Move now, I'm not going to tell you again. Why do you always have to be a nag? Just let me be." But Sasha shed tears as she said, "No" again.

I pulled her off the seat, and she fell on the rocks we had in our front yard and landed on her wrist, hurting herself. I immediately saw my chance to escape, and I jumped on my hog, fired it up, and left. All I could hear as I rode away were my children's screams, and they saw the tears rolling down Sasha's face as she got up to go inside the house. I was already on my way! That demon of addiction had gotten the best of me, and I couldn't even see it. It had jumped on my back, and I couldn't get it off. I was willing to hurt the ones I love for a two second rush. I was willing to make bad memories for my children by the things they saw or heard. I was willing to spend time doing drugs with strangers and drinking with unknown people at their homes instead of being with my family. I was willing to make bad decisions for a high. I was willing to lose my life for a high and lose my family for whatever the cost would be. Did I have a problem? I sure did! A big one!

But I didn't know how to get help. Instead, I just continued being a bulldozer, hurting and running over my loved ones who got in my way. Friend, I blinked, and not months but years had gone by. So much pain I sowed in the people I love, and I was never going to get that back. Once that pain is released to our family, we can't get it back. We just hope they can heal from it.

That next morning, all I could think was how could I have hurt my love? How could I have hurt my kids? How could I have done this? You know what I am talking about, right? We call it the "morning of regrets." It is when all these things begin to replay in our heads. We have times of shame, guilt, and embarrassment. There were many times I told myself that I didn't plan for my life to be this way, but this is where I was. What are we going to do with our lives in this moment? I believe it just doesn't only help our present but also shapes our future. But when we ignore all the warning signs, things slowly start to fall apart in our lives.

I know you see so much honesty in this thought. I have my share of mistakes. I have said things I am ashamed of and have done things I wish I never did. You have to ask yourself right now! "Do I have a problem? Am I really an addict? Can my life continue this way?"

If you have gotten this far in the book, please listen to me, friend. GET HELP NOW! You have NOTHING. I repeat, NOTHING to be embarrassed about. I know your first thought is, "What are people going to say?" "What are people going to think?" Here is some good wisdom: who cares what people think? It's your life, not their's. It's your family, not their's. Here is something else you are thinking, "I provide for my family. I have to work" Listen to me. If you don't get help, your family will lose you for eternity! You need to get better. Please don't waste years trying to get better on your own, just like I did. Please don't say, "I can do this on my own. I don't have a problem." Analyze your life! How many people have you hurt? How many lies have you told? How many broken promises have you made? How many times have you said, "I promise I will change?"

If our families are suffering; if we have to muster up the strength to get by work; if we hurt our loved ones, lie, steal, cheat, spend money on alcohol and drugs without thinking of the consequences; if we can't quit on our own cold turkey, we are addicts, and we need to get the help we need to kick this! Friend, it's okay to ask for help. It's okay to acknowledge that we have been defeated. That pride will eat you alive, trust me!

I did it for years! Somehow, we have to let go of that pride and say I will do what I can to get better.

Are you an addict? Only you know the answer to that question. But before we get into thought 3, you need to know I believe in you! I am your biggest fan, and I am cheering you on to a road of recovery. The truth is I am not special, but I have seen the darkness. I have seen the pain and struggles addictions bring. I have dealt with my demons head-on. I was really good at covering up my life on the outside, but I was bleeding inside. I was slowly dying inside. Inside, I was screaming for help, and I didn't know who to turn to. I had bled all over too many people for too long. My family was suffering, and I didn't even want to see the help. This was because my ego was more important than my recovery. My addiction was more important than my family. Are you an addict?

Much love,
Anthony Torres

Depression will not win me anymore,

and you can't let it win you either.

LETTER 5

Thoughts about
'Depression and Me'

One morning, I woke up unmotivated, unhappy, really down, and heavy. I didn't want to do anything. I was crawling within my own skin for some reason. I wanted to hide in a hole and stay there till this heaviness passed. I wanted to turn off my phone and be disconnected from everyone. I am not sure you ever woke up like that; just heavy and not ready for the day. I mean, who wakes up like that when we are supposed to have joy in our hearts. Everyone in the house was getting to me, and it wasn't them. It was me. It was my mind taking me to places I have never been before. Why was I feeling this way? Keep in mind that I had this feeling while I was serving in the church, and it was after we had had a powerful Sunday.

I understand what depression feels like now versus what it felt like 10 years ago. And now, I understand what it really is: it's a spiritual battle. I am not sure if you're a believer, and it's absolutely okay if you're not. What I want to say will make sense either way.

A guy named Paul in the Bible had a thorn on his side (As probably a physical or emotional thing that God allowed him to go through). As a matter of fact, David said in

Psalm 42:5 *"Why are you downcast, O my soul? Why so disturbed within me?"*

It sounds like he was in a deep emotional state. *Why are you downcast, O my soul?* It was like the writer was saying, "Hey you! What's going on with you? You are not supposed to feel this way." To the point that the writer said, "Okay, now, it's disturbing within me." The point is we all deal with some kind of emotions that we go through on a day-to-day basis—Christian or not. And I wonder how many times we have let those thoughts overshadow our mind to the point of allowing that heaviness to sit on our chest, and we take our own lives because we feel it is the only way out. Because we think it has become too heavy for us to bear

Mental health will allow us to be something we don't understand. How can people with all the money in the world and so much joy take their own lives? Pastors with growing churches, making a difference in the world, speaking into people's lives end up taking their own lives. My depression is mild, and I cope with it. I learn about it, and I keep on. I understand it's not mine to carry anymore but His. I trust Him. If He can help me continue to stay clean and sober, He can help me out with whatever emotional state I deal with.

We think that only weak people deal with depression, and this is not true. Some of the most well-known and successful people also deal with depression. I think it's just a secret we keep to ourselves in fear of what others will think. Charles Spurgeon once said, "I, of all men, am perhaps the subject of the <u>deepest depression</u> at times." There is some pretty depth right there. I am thankful for his transparency and that of other respected people who have stepped forward to admit they battle depression sometimes. It makes us feel like we are not alone in this battle, and you're not alone, friend.

The purpose of writing this thought is that depression does not have to be your identity. It does not have to control your life, and masking it with drugs and alcohol does not make it any better; it's just a different mask. Didn't we forget? We forgot we were depressed because we were high and drunk all the time. It was like that for that moment, and we just didn't think about it. We didn't care. In that moment, some of us were free or became an emotional wreck. Most of the time, deep-rooted emotions and being drunk don't mix in any way. But I am always reminded that what comes up will eventually come down, and sometimes, we come down hard.

I think being depressed and drinking more can trigger more thoughts that can spiral us down a miserable road. It's harder to fight depression when we are sober. We are then forced to deal with it head-on, like a collision. But we must break through that!

Friend, your depression can't be your trigger anymore. You have to find new healthy ways! New thinking! And let me just say this. If you still deal with depression today, there is nothing wrong with you! Yes, people don't understand it. Let's be honest. Sometimes, we don't even understand it either. Yes, people will judge you. Yes, people will have something to say, but remember, it's not who you are. It's not your identity! I get you, friend, and I want this thought to help you somehow. I feel like people with depression feel trapped, lost, and misunderstood. I think what can make a depressed person feel more depressed is trying to explain it to someone who doesn't understand it or overlooks depression. Don't waste your energy trying to explain your depression to others. Use that energy for your day and keep fighting for another day.

Depression is so heavy and dark; it is that emotion we can't turn off and on. It just comes and goes like a dark storm getting ready to set over us. It's like a lion's roar, just waiting for the perfect time to see how loud it can get in our lives. It wants its presence to be known, but don't let that roar be more deafening than God's voice. Shout back if you have to! Speak up! Say, "Nope! Not today! You won't get the best of me today," "Today, you won't win."

I know how I deal with depression these days, and it might look different than you. When I get in that emotional state, I deal with it in healthy ways. I don't go drowning myself in Crown and coke or Bud Light. I don't pop pills or snort coke till my eyeballs pop out anymore. I don't smoke ice or hop on my motorcycle to escape and try to kill myself anymore.

Now when my depression comes upon me, I find healthy ways to press through. I read, I pray, watch movies or workout. I do things to keep my mind busy, to keep my body going. I make sure I don't completely shut down or stay down in that emotion for to long. What ever you need to do, you need to find ways to get through your depression. Keep fighting!

Depression will not win me anymore, and you can't let it win you either. I hope it will go away for me one day, but it's just Jesus and me till then. He knows me and loves me right where I am. And when I say, "Why are you downcast, O my soul?" He strengthens my soul. He holds onto my soul. He speaks to the depth of my soul. If you're a follower of Christ, let me just shout this from the rooftop, "Depression does not make you less Christian," and if you're not a Christian, let me say, "This does not make you less human."

Friend, we need to hang on that we can have HOPE. The hope of seeing that sunshine again someday. One day of saying, "I was down and out, but now I am back doing what I love to do."

My hope is in Christ. What is your hope in? I have talked to many people who feel God doesn't love them because they're depressed. They feel that the cloud will never lift. But on days I feel down, I know tomorrow is a new day. Don't let us allow depression to drag us down; let it strengthen our legs so we can rise back up! See it as a workout for your soul. Every knee bent is strengthening your soul and spirit.

I understand you probably have been dealing with depression for a very long time, and you're afraid to get sober and clean because you think it will get worse. Don't believe that lie! It will only keep you stuck in your cycle of using. You will blink, and 5 to 10 years will go by. It is okay to see a counselor, pastor, someone you can trust and share your feelings with. We have to go places we don't use drugs or alcohol as a cover-up for our emotions, for those deep emotions that nobody understands. We have to somehow come to a place of healing, a place of peace, a place we can healthily deal with depression.

Why this thought? Remember, it's not your identity. You're not whatever you're dealing with emotionally. And I want you to know you are not alone in the battle of depression. You don't have to let it control your life, thoughts, or relationships anymore. I think when we go through this cycle of emotions, we feel we are all alone. I want you to make up your mind that you will find healthy ways to cope with it and press forward in life. We need you! Your family needs you!

Depression has taken many of our brothers and sisters. Even in the church, it has taken great leaders. How many times a year have I read an article of a pastor committing suicide because he was depressed? How many times have you heard of a friend, coworker, or ex-schoolmate doing the same? I wish I could give you more answers on why this happens, but I am sharing what I feel and know from my personal experience. I know you are tired. So am I! I know you're wondering how tomorrow will be. So am I. But you got this, friend! Let's get on that road of recovery and live your purpose-given life.

I wish every person who took their life due to depression could have understood how much they were loved. Maybe they could have seen a different way out of their pain or struggles. Depression doesn't have to break you. It doesn't have to take you; you take it by the horn and fight another day. Fight for peace. Fight to stay sober and clean. Fight for your life. Remember, it is not your identity; don't let it control your life.

Much love,
Anthony Torres

LETTER 6

'ROAR OF MENTAL HEALTH'
(RECITE IT OUT LOUD)

I can hear you!
But my Jesus
Why are you following me?
But my Jesus
You don't scare me!
But my Jesus
You have a grip on me today
But my Jesus
That cloud is getting darker
But my Jesus
I feel like I'm walking through a puddle of water
But my Jesus
Why is everyone staring at me?
But my Jesus
Why is my heart beating fast?
But my Jesus
Why do I feel like I'm going to die today?
But my Jesus
Why do I feel so down?
But my Jesus
I don't feel motivated today

But my Jesus
I don't feel like being social today
But my Jesus
I feel like no one wants me here
But my Jesus
You will never understand me
But my Jesus

When those emotions get louder, when that heaviness starts to set, you may not have the words to say, but your tears and soul will always cry out. BUT MY JESUS!

Much Love,
Anthony Torres

Warning always comes before

destruction

LETTER 7

Thoughts about
'WHAT IS GETTING YOUR ATTENTION?'

One morning, I found myself waking up uneasy and with sweats all over my body. My pillow was soaked as I began to burst into tears at 7 a.m. With panic, Sasha rolled over and said, "What's wrong? Are you okay?" "I had a dream of my grandparents," I replied. I could feel their touch and love, hear their voices, and feel their presence in the dream. I'm sure we've all had dreams like that, where some things felt so real, and we couldn't shake them off.

My grandpa was a medium-built man with a thick mustache that would poke my little cheek and tickle me when he kissed me. My grandma was a slim lady with the sweetest voice I have ever heard. In the dream, my grandpa was sitting on a couch, and my grandma walked in as I was sitting at the table. She began to approach me, and when she got closer, she spoke to me in Spanish, but I couldn't understand what she was saying. I looked at my grandpa, confused. My grandma then came closer and touched my face. I could feel her touch and love. I looked at her hands, and I could see the rings she was wearing in an old picture we took together. She began to speak again in Spanish as she walked away with deep concern on her face. With every word she spoke, she would frown, and

37

I could feel the pain in her voice. But what was she trying to tell me? I kept saying, "I don't understand what you're saying."

That was when I woke up, panicked. I was confused about what I just dreamt about. It was so real! But why? I have never experienced anything like that ever in my life. Why would they visit me this way? Was the God I did not believe in trying to communicate something to me? I was the first grandson, and my grandparents and I were inseparable, like peas and carrots. But they were taken away from me by a drunk driver, killed instantly in a head-on car accident. My mom described that day as the longest and hardest day of her young life.

After collecting my thoughts, I called my mom and told her about my dream. She said, "God is trying to get your attention somehow. He knew how much you meant to them and how much they meant to you. Obviously, you're not listening to me or anyone else. Something in your life needs to change, and he sent your grandparents to get a message across. Figure it out, kid, and turn your life around."

At that moment, I began to think, "Will my addiction kill me? Will I hurt someone? Will I end up in prison? What will my life become?" At that time, I didn't know because I didn't believe in God, but I do know now. God can speak to us in our dreams because sometimes, that's the only time he can get our attention. Let's be honest. We get to a point in our addiction where we don't want to listen to anyone. We couldn't care less about what people say or think about our lives. When people would tell me, "You need to get your life in order," I would say, "You need to mind your own business and worry about your own life." But we all get to a place where we hear no one's voice, not even ours. We do our own thing, hurting anyone that gets in our way. We say things we regret and do things we wish we could get back.

But let me ask you these questions: What has been getting your attention? Did you lose your marriage? Did you end up in the hospital? Did you overdose? Did you wreck your car? What?

Is being in rehab getting your attention? Is being away from your family getting your attention? I think in our life, something has to get our attention to the extent that we say, "Something in my life needs to change." When you drive at 100 miles per hour (mph) with no direction, guidance, or plan in place, you're bound to hit a wall.

Listen, I wanted to DIE an addict! Think about how sad that sounds. Think about how heavy and dark I felt. I was okay with death due to addiction. I would use more drugs, hoping not to wake up anymore! I was willing to lose everything, even my life, to be set free from this addiction. To be set free from this demon —this demon that would torment, blind, and laugh at me. Did I create so much darkness in my life that I couldn't see a way out? I didn't know if I could come out of this. I was stuck like a truck stuck in the mud, spinning its wheels but going nowhere. Have you ever felt like this? Stuck!

That was me, I was spinning my wheels in the cycle of addiction, and I was tired. After the dream featuring my grandparents, it's not like I had a moment I felt like I needed to stop right away. I just realized something needed to change. I mean, that could have been anything in my life. What was causing me the most pain? What was causing my life to fall apart? But I was ignoring the warning signs. They were all around me, and I ignored them. Eventually, those warning signs destroyed me, altered my life, and changed my family. Addiction just doesn't affect you; it affects everything around you, everything it touches

Here is a thought, "Warning always comes before destruction." I ignored everything, and in the end, my whole life fell apart to the point that I had nothing. I was like an 18-year-old kid starting my life all over again. I wasted years I can never get back

Remember, I didn't think I had a problem. I was a functioning addict. Listen to whatever is getting your attention. I hope you will look a little deeper than I did. I hope you will see the warning signs all around you. I hope you will do your homework because I sure didn't. I hope you will stop and think about your life and family because I didn't. I hope it doesn't get so bad for you that you look back and say, "Why didn't I change some things in my life?" You may feel like it now, but it's not too late for you! If you're still breathing, that's called life. It's not over for you yet; you can begin to change things now.

For change to occur, we have to see if there are things in our lives that are getting our attention. I know what that looked like for me. But what does that look like for you? What is speaking to you as you read this? I will end this thought short because I want you to think and write some things down below. WHAT ARE YOUR WARNING SIGNS? Process them and start changing some things in your life to get on this road to recovery.

_____

_____

_____

_____

Okay, do you see what you wrote? Start working on them. Start here! I wonder what my life would look like if I had started cleaning it up after that dream. I probably would have saved my family a lot of heartaches. I think the problem in our lives is we don't think some things can happen to us; we think things like, "Oh, that happened to Joe on TV. He lost everything in his life, but it can't happen to me. I am smarter than that."

One time in Oklahoma, my cousin became addicted to drugs, which broke me because we were so close. At that time, I was flirting with drugs but not near losing control yet (so I thought). I remember searching the streets for her, and little did I know that I would be searching for myself years later. Remember, warning always comes before destruction. The signs are there; how long will we ignore them?

Much love,
Anthony Torres

Because what is broken can be

fixed.

LETTER 8

THOUGHTS ABOUT
'WE ALL HAVE A PAST, CAN WE BE FIXED?'

When I was a little boy, I remember waking up to my parents yelling at each other and the sound of things being thrown against the wall. I was thirsty, and I remember my orange juice was next to my bed, but it had a fly floating in it. I saw what looked like red and blue lights flashing through my window. So I got up and looked out the window, and it was the police. My mom came in with tears in her eyes and her hands shaking. My parents often fought; sometimes it was civil, and sometimes it wasn't. I don't hold that against them because we all have been there before. Lord knows Sasha and I have not had many healthy fights back in the day. We are not taught how to. But I have seen things as a child that still scare me to this day. It's an image that is imprinted on the back of my mind. I have heard things with my innocent ears that I wish I had never heard.

Coming from a divorced family has had its unsettling presence in my younger years and made me asked several questions. Was this normal? Was I the only kid dealing with this? Why did other kids have their parents at award days, and how come I couldn't have mine?

Divorce leaves its scars and unanswered questions written on the hearts of children; it did that to me. Kids tend to think, *Did I cause this? Will my parents get back together?*

As a child, I would dream, looking out the window, seeing my dad drive up with the sunset behind him in the cool crisp fall. He then runs into the house, holds everyone, and says, "Let's get our family back together." He hugs my mother and says, "We will work this out."

Well, at least, this was my dream while growing up anyway, and it never happened. Something inside us just rips us apart; it's a lonely feeling, yes. But I think it's a void that is in every child. Every child deserves to have their parents together, but sometimes life does not always turn out that way. I love stepdads and stepmoms because they try to fill that void that was left, and I am forever grateful for my stepdad today. But let's be honest, nothing fills that void like our biological mother or father. I don't care how old we are; everyone needs their mom and dad.

After years of sobering up, my dad called me on a Wednesday night, we had just gotten out of the church, and I preached that night. He said, "Son, I just watched you minister. You're really good at it, and I am so proud of you." With tears in my eyes, I said, "Thank you, Dad." Keep in mind that I was 32 when this happened. I am sure I had heard those words before, but coming from my dad, it meant so much to me. I had been waiting for him to say those words to me for so long. Every child wants to make their parents proud of them.

To this day, I don't deal with rejection really well, and I am very insecure. This is because, while growing up, I thought I was never good enough for anything or anyone. Maybe you have said these words, "I am a screwup", "I always mess everything up". I said those many times while growing up. I always felt like I never did anything right

One thing that still affects me to this day is losing my grandparents at the hands of a drunk driver in 1986. I bet they would never have thought their grandson would soon turn into a drunk, then get behind the wheel and drive with his family in it. Do we see a trend here? Do we see how history could have repeated itself with my family or another?

Growing up on Wade Street in Las Cruces, NM, behind the projects wasn't so bad. I got in trouble here and there, hung around the wrong crowds, fought, smoked weed at a young age, and began to experiment with alcohol at the age of 14. I thought I was trying to be that cool kid hanging around gang members. Even to this day, I chuckle inside because I was trying to fit in with the crowd. Growing up, I think I went through 5 different stages of who I really was, how I dressed, and how I talked. I think every young kid goes through that. Trying to find yourself as a kid can be challenging, and sometimes it can even be more challenging as an adult.

I started using heavy drugs when I was 17, and the drinking had gotten worse. I was told what every young person doesn't want to hear when they are having sex, "You're going to be a dad!" As I type this, it's hard for me to picture that because I have a 17-year-old daughter. When I was Iliana's age, I found out I was going to be a dad. When I was Bella's age, I was a dad, and when I was Angie's age, I was already going to be a dad for a second time. After having Iliana, I was already addicted to cocaine. I couldn't stop drinking, not even for my kids' sake. They would now be born into my mess. I was the party of the group, and I was okay with that. I was the party animal with a lot of responsibilities that I neglected.

I made a lot of mistakes while growing up and did things I am ashamed of. But one mistake that brought me down to the lowest part of my life was this. Understand that I was a very sexually active young man while growing up, and I wish I wasn't. Before Illiana was born, I had gotten someone else pregnant, knowing I would be a father again with someone else, it was something that couldn't happen. I was so young, dealing with so many responsibilities.

I wasn't ready for my first child; how could I be ready for another with a different woman? So I buckled, and I was in a position that I thought I would never be in, granting someone life or death. With much selfish talk, we both decided to have an abortion. And since that day, I emotionally spiraled out of control, knowing I worked overtime to pay for it. Every dollar that came in was not to grant someone life; it was to end it.

It was abortion day, going to the clinic is something that is still real to me. Even in 2021, I can feel all those emotions that go along with doing something like this. There were probably 10 women packed in that place, and I could sense that escape from them all. You could see those that had uncertain and scared faces like us. Those faces of "I have been here before." One lady we were sitting next to told us it was her fourth time being there. She was a prostitute on the streets. But she talked, and her body language spoke that this was something she was okay with. It was just a part of her routine. Even though light came through the windows, as the minutes wasted away, so did my soul. As the light shined, it got darker in that waiting room.

It was our turn and I didn't go back with her, I waited, with all those emotions balled up in one. She came out with her head down, and I grabbed her hand, wishing this never happened. It's not like we walked out, skipping with smiles on our faces. No! We walked out in pain, disgust, and wondered what in the world we just did. You can try to cover up some things, but you can't just ignore them.

I can't speak for her about how she felt all these years ago, nor how it impacted her. It's been 22 years since we last spoke, but I can tell you the impact that action had on me spiritually. It damaged me in every way it can and could. Know that spirits are attached to some things, and when that happened, I believe I lost my heart and spirit once that little one's life was cut short. And knowing I played a part in that caused me to bleed inside. I thought about it all the time. When bad things would happen, I would sit and think this so-called God was punishing me. Nothing ever went right in my life because of what I did.

This was too much for an 18-year-old! How could I? That was probably one of the most selfish things I could have ever done in my life. Even to this day, I wonder what they would have looked like. I wonder what they would have become. I wonder what a great life they would have had or what profession they would have chosen. I didn't even give them a chance to live at all because of my selfish act. They never stood a chance because of my actions, and I beat myself up over that. I was very young, and it's a mistake I regret even to this day.

It caused me a lot of emotional pain and tears in my life. Many people don't know this, but I would cry my eyeballs out and ask for forgiveness from them if they could hear me from heaven. My spirit would be forever damaged, and my heart never healed from that until the day I gave my heart to Christ. He began to heal those areas of my life (slowly). We can't go back to the past; it's just our emotional scars we revisit from time to time. But He can, and for that, I am thankful. Even as I write this, I still feel that heaviness, but it's not mine to carry anymore. I know I have been forgiven for what I did, but I would never want anyone to go through that again. There is something mysterious that is spiritually attached to it. But what can be broken can be fixed!

I know some of you who know me are saying, "I never knew this about you." Well, it's not like I shout it from the rooftop. I am embarrassed about it, but I brought it to light with the hope of helping someone healthily process their emotions. I truly believe there are emotional scars and battles that we try to shove under the rug. We get a feeling that when we don't talk about some things, they really never happened! But we can all agree that it truly never goes away till we learn to deal with it healthily. We face it head-on, and we truly find that we can heal from whatever has scared us as a child or young adult. This also applies to relationships or every damage that has been done, either self caused or natural.

I also remember I was molested a few nights as a child by a family friend, but I don't think it affected me while growing up, other than the fact that I could never trust anyone or take people's word for it.

When you tell someone, "NO! Don't touch me there," and they still do it anyway, you feel helpless. When it happens again because they know they got away with it the last time, you cry and tell them to stop, but they continue to touch you. You realize your little body is no match for their sweaty, over-sized body. Inside, you feel nasty, abused emotionally, and they took something from you that you can never get back. I never said anything because I knew I would not stay at that house anymore. We were just staying there because we were traveling. Besides, I didn't think anyone would believe me. I probably should have said something, who knows how many kids this person hurt or how much emotional trauma they caused?

Brokenness comes in all different shapes and forms in our lives. Maybe your life was awful all the way from your youth; I don't feel mine was bad. I had people who loved and challenged me, but I have my scars as a young person, whether it was because of something I did or an event life altered. You may be wondering how I survived getting raped, getting beaten, being abused. Relationship after relationship, being abandoned by my parents, foster home after foster home, hurt after hurt. Again, I don't feel my life was so bad, but I do wish it was different in some ways. I think everyone can say that, but being broken is being broken; pain is pain. And we wonder if we can ever be fixed. Can we ever heal in certain areas of our lives, or is it always going to be this way? Will I always be this way? Will my thinking always be this way? Will my guard always be up? Will I ever let anyone in? Can I love again?

Did you know most of the daily struggles of 80% of the people I counsel stem from how they grew up and how they were treated as children? Low self-esteem, insecurity, and trust are just some of the things people struggle with. You have those struggling with addictions. Is it to numb the pain? Is it to erase that bad memory? Is it not to feel anymore?

Right now, I know you think you can't be fixed. You think you can't be healed. You think you can't beat this addiction. You think you're always going to be stuck in your past, but that's all it is! It's your past. Listen to this; it's hard to get to your future if you're always looking behind you. It's hard to get to a place of healing if you're always opening up those old wounds again. I hope you can heal one day. I hope one day, you can let go of your past. I hope you see yourself not as this monster or a lost cause but as someone who is loved, needed, and has a purposeful life. I hope you see that your past was not meant to break you but help you today to be stronger in life. All those areas of your life you have been keeping people from can heal. All those thoughts that you feel control you and have gotten the best of you can heal! I truly believe today is going to be a new day for you! Your past does not define who you are today.

If you are reading this, it's not over for you yet! Let's get ready to heal your past. Let's get ready to have this new life. I am praying for you today, and remember I am your biggest fan cheering you on because I believe in you. Let's go! Because what is broken can be fixed.

Much love,
Anthony Torres

You will leave me here in my mess,

darkness, and puddle of emotions

LETTER 9

THOUGHTS ABOUT
'YOU WILL KILL ME, WON'T YOU?'

I got up one morning like I had cheated on my wife with you; the guilt was so heavy, like a weight of bricks laying down on me. You kept me up all night, with me doing most of the talking. I got lost in my thoughts, and you didn't even say a word. You just let me ramble on about life! I got lost in my thought of hopelessness. My wife will leave me if she finds out about you! You must not show up when she is around. You will kill me, won't you?

My relationship with you is different from any other. As a matter of fact, it was a relationship that didn't start off slow. I just jumped right in, and I knew it was love right off the bat. Do you remember? You loved me right where I was. You didn't look down on me or judge me. You just let me right in! You would always make me feel that everything was going to be okay! I still remember our first night! I felt secure and accepted. You made all my worries go away. You made all the pain that I had been stuffing down for so long start to fade away. That tree that once had dead leaves was now forming new ones. It got to the point that all I wanted to do was spend time with you. When I was away from you, I felt lost and empty. I have never felt this way before. You got me, and you were the only one who understood me! But you will kill me, won't you?

I haven't seen you in 3 days, and it's killing me. Why do I need you around? Why do I need you in my life? I have a great job and family. Am I willing to throw away everything I have for our secret? I am finding myself angry. I am like a roach pacing back and forth. I need to get in contact with you. NO! That will cause problems. What do I do? I feel all those feelings beginning to build up again. I need to see you soon! But you will kill me, won't you?

My secret is out now; she knows, and so does everybody else, but I can't stop seeing you! I feel like I will lose myself if I stop. If I stop, I won't know how to handle myself. You keep me in check. My mind is where it needs to be. Why won't you listen to me when I talk? Why won't you say anything back? Why is it that I need more of you to keep me going? Can't I just be satisfied and happy with a little bit of your time, a little bit in how you make me feel? I know you have to go! So do I! But you will kill me, won't you?

At this moment, I can't stand the sight of you. I can't stand how you make me feel! Why is this happening? Why are you doing this to me? Why are you now allowing me to hurt? How could our relationship start off so well and now going to end so badly? Not for you, but for me! You will move on to someone else, and you will be someone else's little secret, won't you?

What about me? What happens to me? You will leave me here in my mess, darkness, and puddle of emotions. You don't care about me; you never did. Why are you now following me? You didn't speak much then, but I can hear you speak now! Stop playing games with me! Why won't you let me move on so that we can go our separate ways? Why won't you let our relationship end in peace? You're making this really hard for me. You will kill me, won't you?

I'm going to have to call the ambulance because you hurt me badly! You wouldn't leave me alone. I can't breathe. I can't feel my face. My heart that once beat for you is now trying to beat out of my chest. You're killing me. Please stop. I can't breathe! I'm getting pale and hot. My insides are hurting. You're making my skin itch. You're making my hands shake. Why are you making me feel this way? Please stop. Please make all this go away. I trusted you with my feelings, emotions, and life! I lost everything for you, but you will kill me anyway!

I am in my room. I can't move my body, but I can hear voices talking over me. It sounds like the cops and EMT. Why can't I speak? All I can do is listen. They also found out about you. They are taking you away. I feel trapped inside my body. Wait! I now hear a beeping sound. Am I in the hospital? I can feel my arms hurting like I have been poked 10,000 times. I can hear voices again. I can hear people weeping. What do you mean I am not going to make it? 2 weeks! Wait! What? You know I can hear you, right? My body is giving out. How can this be? I knew it! I knew this relationship with you was going to catch up to me. I lost everything, and now I am going to die alone and broken! I should have left you a long time ago, but you had a hold on me, like a crocodile killing its prey. I feel emptier than ever, and I can't believe I let this relationship go on longer and get out of hand. You never cared about me! I had more invested in you than you had in me. I let you get the best of me. I should have said goodbye years ago because, in the end, you did end up killing me anyway!

"You have the shovel in your hands;

let's stop digging that hole deeper"

LETTER 10

THOUGHTS ABOUT
'PEOPLE CAN'T SAVE YOU FROM YOUR ADDICTIONS'

E ven today, it still strikes me how many couples or families lose years over addictions. Time can be lost if the person got addicted while in the relationship or before getting in the relationship. The hardest thing anyone has to do is living with a spouse that is addicted; they have so many questions and so few answers.

Do I leave? Do I stay? How can I help? What do I do? Especially if they have been together for a long time, so many years of investment with kids and careers, and they now find out their spouse is addicted to drugs or alcohol. For a person that is addicted, we just think, "When are they going to leave me?" "Why are they still with me?" It is hard and very challenging for both parties.

If you live with an addicted spouse, I am about to tell you something really hard for you to swallow and accept, but I believe there is a lot of truth in it. You can't save your spouse; you need to release them. It's a tough place to be, and it doesn't mean you have given up on them or don't love them. You care about them so much that you must remove that enabling system so they can truly find themselves. Some things need to change because the old way is not working. Years are being

57

lost! Some might agree or disagree with me because we feel that we are giving up on them, and it will be our fault if something happens to them, but this is not true. We are all responsible for our own actions.

If you're on the other side of the fence, and they let you go, trust me, it wasn't easy for them. But what are you going to do now that your world is starting to turn upside down? I know every bit of emotion you're feeling. It's hard. It's a place I wish to never revisit.

One time, I asked Sasha, "Why did you stay? Eight years of lies, broken promises, unfaithfulness, late night fights. Eight years of hurting you emotionally, and you taking care of me when I got sick because I had been on a two day binge. WHY? Why did you stay, knowing I was going to hurt you again? I was always making you feel like you're nothing."

She said, "I thought I could change you. I thought I could be enough for you. I thought having your daughter and son would be enough. I thought hopefully, soon to be, your wife would be enough," and in the end, it wasn't enough. She had to leave. She had to release me! I had to be in a place I was unfamiliar with, without my family. And just like that, after all the years of pain, she mustered up the strength and left. When I was out in the bars, doing me like I had been doing all those years, she packed up her stuff and the kids' in the middle of the night and left. I am sure it was one of the hardest things she ever had to do in her life. I'm sure she had tears in her eyes with every suitcase she packed. I'm sure as she packed, every fight and harsh words that were spoken in that house stabbed her heart as she remembered them. Her strength began to leave her with every hygiene product she put in zip lock baggies. I'm sure with every sight of the kids' beds being loaded in a truck, her heart broke. The dreams of our used-to-be happy family were shattered! With the confusion on the kids' faces, I'm sure she wept for them because they didn't know why they were leaving. They didn't know where I was! Our family would now be split apart, and a place we called home would be no more due to addictions. And we would be that statistic.

If you released your spouse, I know right now that it is so hard for you because you're watching the one you love kill themself. You're watching the father or mother of your kids being nonchalant.

If you're on the other end, we had to hear people tell us NO at some point in our addiction. "No, you can't stay here." "No, I won't give you money." "No, I won't get your car out of impound." "No, I won't get you out of jail." "No, you can't sleep on my couch." Then we respond with, "Well, I guess you really don't care about me then. I am better off dead!"

Listen, I played the guilt card with people for years; some bought it, and some didn't. But in the end, I needed to do something in my life to see that I could change. I was not getting any better; I was getting worse. I would say stupid things to Sasha: "If you leave me, I will kill myself." "Even if you did leave me, you wouldn't make it on your own. I have all the money," and maybe not so nice, but you get the picture. I was hateful, full of rage and bitterness in my heart. It was dark and ugly! I would tell my parents that if they shut the door on me, I would think they didn't love me. What kind of parents could shut the door on their own son? At that point, I think no one had a clue of what to do with me, and in all honesty, I didn't even know what to do with myself.

And let me just say this, if you're playing the guilt card, don't do it! Your family has so much going on already in adjusting to life without you. I can personally say this adds so much more stress to them. You might think they don't care, and you know that's not true. They don't need to hear, "I'm going to end my life." They need to hear, "I got myself here.

I will get out of this." Imagine more of the pain you will leave them if you did decide to do something to yourself. It's easy to pass blame and guilt on people, but the hardest part for us to do is to muster up the strength to move forward and own up to what we have done or become and get better.

As you're reading this, you're angry at someone that shut the door on you. They turned their back on you. You feel lied to and betrayed. You're upset because they said they would be there, and now, they are not. And yes, it does hurt. But I think it's supposed to hurt or sting a little bit.

I understand your thought process. I hated Sasha for months after she left. Because when I went to rehab, she saw me off like a lost child. She saw me off with tears in her eyes but yet with a look of disgust on her face. It was a look like, "I am sorry it got to this point. I tried to help you." Her wish for me to get the needed help was granted, but in the end, she never wrote back. Her phone calls were short. I thought she would be there at the moment I needed her the most. And she wasn't there for me; the truth is I lost her months ago. She was just hanging on to a fine thread. And at the right time, she was going to cut that string. So I got angry at her and stayed that way for a while. I was in unfamiliar territory, with unfamiliar feelings, and I didn't like it one bit.

Right now, you're in jail, rehab, or somewhere in the world getting better, and your loved one is not in touch with you. They are ignoring you. They're not letting the kids speak to you. You feel alone, betrayed, and abandoned.

But listen to me when I say this, and by all means, I am not trying to make things worse for you. We forced our families into this corner. They're confused, hurt, and trying to process their emotions, just like you are in this situation. Remember, something had to be given, friend, and I am sorry it got to this point in your life. Think about this for a second.

My kids were now back at grandma's house, ripped from their home, rooms, and that place that was safe for them—that place called home. Sasha was now wondering how she was going to pay bills and provide for the kids. I put her in that situation. I forced her to make this move. I forced her to leave me and put herself in an awkward situation. But she did what she had to do to protect her sanity, to protect the kids. Our relationship at this point was toxic, and there was no fixing it anymore. We tried for too long, and as much as it hurt me when she left, I needed to put myself in her shoes. I probably would have done the same thing. Maybe you need to put yourself in their shoes for once, feel what they feel or what they are going through apart from you. When we do this, we look at things just a little bit differently.

You have to allow your family to process these emotions the best way they can, and it might not be how you want it. But it is a process! Right now, at this moment, you have to process these emotions you have honestly and healthily. Those in your circle, your family and friends, must do the same. Everyone in your circle is in a place like you, and they never thought they would be. And at some point, we must force ourselves to look in the mirror and honestly face what we've done. Hear me when I say you can get through this.

At that moment, I never would have said this, but I am glad Sasha did leave me. She finally did it. She dug deep in her soul and got the strength to leave, taking the kids as far away from me as she could, hoping that I would see what I was doing to our family.

But I think it was more for her to begin to heal as a woman and as a mother. For her not to have someone dragging her down so much, belittling her, making her feel so low as she had encountered so much emotional abuse from me. In time, she would need to heal from this season in her life. She would heal from all the pain I had caused her. A woman can only take so much.

I won't go into details about her emotions now or her thought process; that will be another letter for her to share with you. But this is more for you to understand that you can't save yourself, and neither can your family. You have to get to a place where you want to get better! But I believe in you! With the right plan and support system, I'm certain you can be on your way to recovery. This has been going on for too long, friend. You're spinning your wheels in the mud.

We have to get to the lowest place in our life where something clicks in our head to say, "You know what? I need help. I need someone to help me." Hang in there. It will get better!

I'll close this thought with a message for you. Nobody is going to come to your rescue. You have the shovel in your hands; let's stop digging that hole deeper

However, trust me when I say your family hasn't given up on you. They are tired! They can't save you anymore. You have to be at rock bottom to find saving, forgiveness, and healing. Your family must stop throwing the life jacket at you. They must stop enabling you, and it's not that they don't love you anymore. They just want to see you get better. It's up to you to take the proper steps to get better and put on the life jacket daily. Let's get our hearts ready for the next letter.

Much love,
Anthony Torres

"Hope is not something. Hope is in someone! And that's Christ! Start climbing out of the darkness"

LETTER 11

THOUGHTS ABOUT
'5 MINUTES OF DARKNESS'

I f there is anyone who flirted with darkness, it was me. We joke about it as though it is not real. I learned that if the devil can make people think the darkness is not real, we won't need to reach for the light. We then just continue to stay in the dark! There are doors I wished I never opened, the doors that I chose to walk through. My tattoos of demons and Satan mirrored my dark heart once. I was that guy that wanted to get an upside-down cross on my arm and the picture of the pentagram tattooed somewhere on my body. I used to talk with the devil as if he was my best friend. "If you're 555, then I'm 666," sounded cute, coming out of my mouth; it was a line from a song I heard. But the more I said it, the more I believed it. The more I reached for him, the more hardened and dark my heart and life got. To this day, I am thankful I never got that darkness on my skin, and even now, I am trying to do what I can to clean up my body that I once abused with darkness written on me with coverups.

That reflection of the times spent in darkness is a great reminder, but I remember every needle that jabbed my skin. I remember every thought process at that time and moment. I remember every pain and trial in my personal life that came with it. Darkness is a place some will never understand unless you have been there. It's a place of open assault on our mind from the devil, a place of defeat every day. It's a place that we only wish we can come out of, a place of hopelessness. It's a place where we see what we've been holding on to when we claw and scratch. Darkness takes our voice. It paralyzes our ability to move and get out of what we have gotten ourselves into. Darkness is deep, heavy, and evil. When we think of Satan, we think of a guy in a red cap and pitchfork. But he is real. If you have felt that dark presence, you will know what I am talking about.

I was reminded of this one time that I had fallen asleep after being up for three days. My body and spirit needed much rest. As I closed my eyes, I then remember opening them. I was awake in my dream, and I could see Sasha next to me, but I could also sense that someone was walking towards me. When I turned my head, I could see this 6ft shadow coming near me. With every step that he took, I could sense evil. I could sense a battle and a fight for my body and soul. The closer he got, the more scared I got. Do you remember seeing a scary movie with your parents when you were young? You were scared when you went to bed and decided that you wouldn't use the restroom when you woke up in the middle of the night, regardless of how full your bladder was. If your mom told you to go turn off the light in the hallway, you would muster up the courage to do it and run as if your little life depended on it. You swore it felt like someone was chasing you as hair stood up on the back of your neck.

I was getting that same feeling as an adult! The person was chasing me, and he wouldn't leave me alone! Then, there he was, standing over me. I couldn't see his face; all I could sense was his presence. He was so close to me that if it was cold, I would be able to see his breath. He then began to reach for me, and my heart beat fast, and my body felt like I had pins and needles entering me and that feeling of a rock on top of me. I couldn't hold this feeling inside me anymore. I needed help. He was suffocating me! Again like a child, I mustered up the strength to yell, and when I tried to yell, "SASHA, HELP!" Nothing came out. "HELP! HELP!" I tried again, but nothing still was coming out. They were empty words. As my mouth was moving, it was like Satan had taken my voice.

Even more afraid, I tried to reach for Sasha, and I couldn't move. My whole body was now paralyzed by this 6ft evil spirit, by this darkness. He was keeping me stuck in that moment. And I yelled again, but I found myself actually waking up from the scream. With sweat running down my face and with deep breaths of panic, I was awake, and I could now move. I'm telling you, friend, it was real.

The scientific term for this is "sleep paralysis." It sounds cute, but I don't believe it. Darkness and evil are in this world, and they're in people's hearts. If we have to dismiss evil spirits, then we have to dismiss God altogether. Why was this happening to me? Well, I believed I had opened doors I should have never opened. I was flirting with darkness, and it was letting me know how real it was. I would have those dreams often, and it seemed more when I had been on drugs. I read a book by a well-known baseball player who was an addict and dealt with the same dreams. Was there a pattern here? Were addicts dealing with this same issue? Was the devil trying to torment us because we have become so vulnerable to using drugs and poisoning our hearts and mind? What was it?

Maybe you have been down in the dark for too long. Maybe you think your heart is so dark that you don't think there is any good in you. Maybe you have had these dreams as well. I think about them now and how much they scared me to think that there was something bigger than me. I am a grown man, and even when I think about it, I still get goosebumps on my arm. Darkness is real! Because when you play with fire, you will eventually get burned. When you open those doors of darkness, you will eventually find it and get lost in it.

Since I started following Christ, I can say that I haven't had those dreams since. It is because I am reminded that in darkness, the light will always shine again. I am reminded that no matter how many times I have flirted with darkness, no matter how many times I got stuck in darkness, the light shines brighter

Maybe you feel darkness is overshadowing you. Maybe you feel like there is no hope for you in the dark. Demons are real, and I truly believe they torment us in so many ways. But they don't have a hold over me anymore because the God I serve is real and bigger than anything I face. There is hope for you in the dark, and there is hope for you amid your demons. I will get preachy on you in one sentence. Hope is not something. Hope is in someone! And that's Christ! Start climbing out of the darkness

Much love,
Anthony Torres

"What is your enough? How will people remember you?"

LETTER 12

THOUGHTS ABOUT
'WHEN ENOUGH IS ENOUGH'

One morning, Sasha had left, and I was going on two weeks of trying to figure some things out in my life. This was probably when it would be the turning point for me to change. Have you ever felt just tired? I am talking about tired of fighting yourself. You see the black, tired eyes, bloodshot eyes, bruised, bloody knees, and chapped knuckles. Like you know deep down inside that you need to put some things in order. This would be one of those days for me in my life.

That morning, I needed more cocaine, and my dealer lived in Doña Ana. I had my last 40 dollars in my pocket, and I had already started selling stuff just to satisfy my high; it was getting bad very quickly for me. I decided to jump on my motorcycle as this was my last means of transportation. But as I was riding to Doña Ana, I got on the highway, and a car cut me off to get to the side road. I saw the car, and I hit my brakes, which caused the bike to fishtail. With my heart racing, just knowing I would feel my death, I hit the back of his car with my bike, which bounced me back to an upright position, with me still trying to maintain control. The next thing I knew was my upper chest was over the handlebars. As I began to slow down, there I was, staring at the pavement. When I examined my bike, the only thing that was damaged was my crash bars that bent, and my front wheel cover was scratched. I had only sprained my wrist from getting smashed. I really could not believe what just occurred. Why was I still alive?

What in the world just happened? I had been riding bikes long enough to know that this just does not happen. I know many bikers who had gone down on their bikes by simply turning and hitting a patch of sand. I hit the back of a car! I hit the back of the car due to lack of sleep and still drunk and high from the night before. I really should have been dead. I never rode without a helmet which would have made my fall off the bike more damaging to my body with injuries or even death

Listen to me; this does not happen! The driver just kept going and didn't stop. It probably was a good thing because I would have gone to jail that day even if it wasn't my fault. But it didn't stop me from what I felt I needed to go and get. I was on a cocaine mission, and nothing was going to get in the way of that.

After getting what I needed in Doña Ana, I went back home and snorted the whole bag of cocaine in less than an hour. I got desperate and needed more! I crushed some pills I had and snorted those also. I drank and sang. I was all by myself in that house, a sad and misunderstood soul that was slowly wasting away.

I remember playing guitar hero then running to the blinds because I was paranoid the cops were looking for me. I was paranoid for some reason like someone was chasing me, and I didn't even know why. I had a run-in with the Gang task force officer the night before; maybe this was what triggered it. He stopped me for speeding but seemed to be more interested in my club colors than anything, and with the amount of drugs I had in my pocket. If he had searched me, I would have been sent to jail for a while, but luckily he let me go.

That day after more of using (drugs), it hit me really hard. My body had just had enough, and it was letting me know real quick. It was at the tipping point of shutting down. My heart began to beat fast, and I was sweating so much that the top of my shirt was getting wet. I couldn't breathe; my breath began to get smaller. I felt like I couldn't get enough air into my lungs, and I gasped for air. I began to get dizzy and light-headed.

So I went outside to get some air, and I opened my phone to see the picture of my son and his curly hair. I had not seen him in some days. My son needed his father, and my actions said I would rather get high than spend time with my boy. He needed his dad, but I was not right in my own mind to be around him or the girls.

I felt like I was literally going to fall over and die, and for once in my life, I was afraid. This was it; I had finally done it. I was going to die from my addiction and live in hell forever. My soul didn't belong in heaven. I felt like I needed to call 911, but I was afraid because I had drugs in the house.

I called Sasha to tell her that I felt like I was overdosing and I would die. And to see if she could come get me and take me to the hospital. She was my last hope. She had been there for me before, and she would be there for me again. I was sure of it, but her response shocked me. She said, "No." Okay, wait a second, she just told me no. ARE YOU KIDDING ME?

She said, "I have been there for you for eight years. Always bailing you out. Always there for you! Always picking up the pieces of our lives. No, I am not coming."

I told her, "I'm going to die in my addiction alone, and you don't care."

She said, "Anthony, I have done all I can for you, figure it out. You're not my problem anymore. I got kids to worry about," and she hung up on me.

With pure shock on my face, shrugging my shoulders back, and a long grasp of breath coming out of my mouth, I went back inside the house. I was not going to call the ambulance; they would call the cops to arrest me. I had drugs in the house, baggies, and beer cans everywhere. The house was smelling like a trash can. So I got a jug of water and began to drink it fast; the water came out from the side of my mouth, spilled on my clothes and out to the floor. My body was getting hot, and my chest was hurting as I felt like I couldn't breathe. So I threw myself in the shower with my clothes still on, my wet jeans stuck to my legs, and my shoes were soaked with water, making funny sounds. I curled up in the corner of the shower, letting the cold water hit my tired face with my eyes plagued with dark circles around them.

I began to slap and hit my face. I wept, and with a loud yell from the depth of my lungs, I screamed! The sound echoing off the broken walls could be heard. I screamed again, "O God, take my life!" I was the scum of the earth, and I did not deserve to live. I begin to shake and cry out more, with pausing moments to collect my thoughts. I began to think, *what in the world was my life becoming*. This was the first time I cried out to God that I was not sure about. In my desperate time of need, I knew I had reached down to the deepest part of my pained heart and needed something more. With minutes passing, I got up, turned the shower off, and stripped my clothes off. But did I learn my lesson in that moment? Of course, not. What was happening to me? As the hours passed, I drank again and licked all of the residues of cocaine off the bags that I had left, and I passed out on the carpet, naked, ashamed, and broken.

I woke up to someone pounding at the door. I must have gotten up, moved to the couch, and covered myself because this was where I was at. As I got up to open the door, my mom, with an upset voice, said, "What are you doing? Where have you been? Everyone has been calling you for the last 15 hours. Sasha and I thought you were dead. Look at this place, it stinks, and you're getting worse; just look at you!" I felt like telling my mom, "I have looked at me for years. Trust me that I hate what I have become."

"ENOUGH IS ENOUGH. You're going to end up killing yourself, and your kids will not have a father. What is wrong with you? Get it together," she said. "This is not how I raised you!" she added with pain in her voice, walked out, and slammed the door behind her.

I know what you're thinking. *What did I do next?* Honestly, I got up, got a beer, smashed some prescription drugs I found, and snorted them. I then laid there on the floor, looking up at the ceiling. I was tired, really tired. Tired of this life, tired of letting people down, tired of not knowing if I would see tomorrow. Just tired! I couldn't do this anymore. She was right; enough was enough, and I needed help. I had been doing this for too long, and for once, I was flat-out tired.

What is your *enough*? At what point in your life did you say, "I'm tired." We have been doing this for too long. Our bodies get tired, and we are unsure of how long we can keep going on like this. Something needs to change, but where do we start? I think that's the starting point for a lot of us.

What is your enough? Losing your kids? Losing your family? In and out of jail, homeless on the streets? What is it? Coming out of a coma after an overdose? A near-death experience or losing a family member to drugs? Wrecking your vehicle?

Your enough will drive you to find help. Your enough will make you realize that all the late nights, blackouts, times you were throwing up, times you couldn't find a vein in your arm to shoot up are not worth it. Your enough will make you see there is more to your life than you think. Your enough will make you search your own soul until you realize that something needs to change. We need to make moves to get there, but what is your enough? I saw mine, and honestly, I was afraid to deal with it. But I knew I had to start somewhere

So I picked up the phone and began to call detox places. I couldn't believe I was at this point in my life. But I was; I needed real help, and enough was enough. I was sick and tired of living this way. I needed to find help immediately, or the truth was my drugs were going to bury me; they were going to be the end of me.

This is not how I wanted to be remembered. This is not how I wanted to end my life. I didn't want to end my story in my addiction. Enough was enough, but was it enough for me to get help? I hope so because I was at the end of my rope. I can say I was truly at the end of me. As you read this, my question for you is, what is your enough? How will people remember you?

Much love,
Anthony Torres

"It's not how you start this life;
it's how you finish it." Let's finish

it strong!"

LETTER 13

THOUGHTS ABOUT
'REHAB'

The other day someone walked into my office, shaking with bloodshot eyes; you could tell they lacked sleep. Their eyes were red as if they had been crying all night. Their body looked like it was ready to give out; it looked like they haven't showered in some days. They wore a look of desperation I had seen before. It was like PTSD for me all over again. I have been here before with myself. It took me back to a place. A place I came from, a place I often go back to with the aim of helping people. The place of hopelessness. A place of pain, a place of darkness, the place that I remember my demons so well as they would torment me. The place of "how did I get here?" A place I once remember checking myself into rehab in mid-August 2009.

Admitting you need help is the hard part; getting to a detox or rehab place is more challenging. Our pride is checked, and our ego is tested. We bother about what people will say people say and think.

Here I was, at the back of my parents' car, with my knees bouncing up and down, and nervousness was written all over my face while they drove me to detox in El Paso, TX. Why were my hands shaking? Was I going through withdrawal? Was I afraid? What was wrong with me? What was going on in my body? Not sure if I even got any sleep the night before. But here I was, taking the biggest step of my life. As I walked through the door, it felt like everyone's eyes were piercing through my face. Like "O another one," or "I wonder how long he will last in here." In my mind, I was like, "Seriously, what are you looking at?"

At a point during the processing, I was tired of all the questions thrown at me. Yes, I am an addict! Yes, I know the last time I used. Will you stop asking me 21 questions and give me my meds and bed so I can sleep this nightmare off? The take-in process was humiliating for me. I became frustrated and angry real quick. It had been 24 hours since I last had one drop of alcohol or drugs in my system. Why was I here? Did I really need to be here? For years, I woke up in the morning to the sound of "Daddy, can I have some breakfast?" to hearing the kids watch cartoons and seeing Sasha getting ready for the day. And here I was, waking up in a room shared with two other guys. A room as hot as Arizona in the summer, where my body was only covered with a small thin sheet. A room that smelled of farts, armpits, and men. I felt like I was in hell and that there was no way to return to the reality of my life.

As the morning came, all I could hear down the hall was a lady yelling "breakfast" and "smoke break." My roommates jumped out of bed. With me wiping the cold out of my eyes, I decided to put my shower shoes on and see what all the commotion was all about. I learned three things real quick in rehab: Coffee, cigarettes, and crossword puzzles are your friends!

I got my weekly schedule which was a lot of classroom/therapy sessions. The smoke break was every other hour. Breakfast, lunch, and dinner were their normal times. Free time was limited with one TV for everyone to watch, and sadly, I missed a pre-season Dallas Cowboy game. With all of us dressed in scrubs and all from different races and backgrounds, we all shared stories of defeat, struggles, pain, and even death!

This one guy lost his friend to an overdose, while this girl on the phone next to me was weeping because she just got a phone call from her lawyer that she lost custody of her kids to the state. This was our new reality of life; things were now changing slowly, and I knew the effect of addiction by hearing others' stories. There was the same pain, struggle, and darkness. But the emotions seem to be the same amongst addicts. Even down to the thought process and in recovery, I heard people say, "This is my second or third time here." I wonder if I would be a repeater, someone who spent their whole life in and out of rehab. I didn't want my life to be that way.

Rehab was hard and challenging for me; it really was! It was a sad, lonely, and hard place to collect your thoughts. I had seen this in a movie before and thought, *Man, it must suck to be that person*, and here I was. Was this me? Am I supposed to be here? Could there have been another way? Rehab was a mix of emotions balled up with physical pain that I will never be able to explain. We all had our moments of emotional breakdown, joy, sadness, and then back down to our reality. Back to our own hell, back to our place of torment, the place of feeling our lowest and being an unfamiliar spot. And I felt stuck! Like really stuck! I was able to do limited things, and I hated every bit of feeling that way. Someone was telling you when to eat, when to get up, what classes to go to, and when to smoke.

But I did my best with what I had, and I adjusted the best I could. I went from smoking Newport to rolling cigarettes and going through books of crossword puzzles daily. I am telling you! They were desperate times. I processed my emotions the best way I could while I was in there. But one day, I ran across something that I thought I would never read. The Bible! I know! I was so far from God, and I am surprised my hands didn't catch fire when I touched the Bible. I literally hated God. I hated him for what he created (me). I hated him for my life. I hated him for every pain he caused me in life. I hated him because when I asked him to "take my life," I was still breathing. I wasn't an atheist, but I was getting close to it. I had my questions about this so-called God.

My creator was my enemy, and I would throw stones at him if I could, hoping they would hit him to get his attention. I was reading a book called Psalms; those writings were pretty deep. My heart had darkened and hardened over the years. It would take a true act of God to get through it. It would take something powerful to change it! I had no care at all. Have you ever gotten to a point in time in your life where you say, "Why am I here?" "What is my purpose?" "What can I possibly do with my life now?" That was me at that moment

But my regret, if I had any, was that I didn't stay all the way through the program. After I transferred out of detox to a rehab place on my third night, I left at 12:30 am. I started walking the streets of El Paso, not knowing where I was going. I had become that guy you walked past on the streets late at night.

I made phone calls, and eventually, someone came to get me. And there I was again, at a bar, drinking and doing cocaine. It was like I never left. It was like the devil was waiting very patiently for me to return. I was back to my place of familiarity, which I created for myself.

I have so much to say about my rehab experience. I have so much to share about why I didn't stay. Addiction is not like a light switch you can turn off. It's not like you go to some classes, hear some people speak, and bam! You're sober and clean a few days later. It requires hard work. Why?

This is because it all depends on you. I would say, and this number is probably pretty high, but 80% of people are in rehab for all the wrong reasons. They aren't there for themselves. They are there because their spouse threatened to leave if they didn't get help. Most are there because of the court's order or because they felt pressured to get help.

If you're reading this, I need you to really hear me on this thought. Why are you there? Are you there because you really want to get better? If you are, you will make it, you will get over this roadblock of addiction, and you will stick out the boring classes, the bedtime curfew, that nasty food, and sharing a room with someone you don't know.

No matter what, you will stick out that uncomfortable spot, and guess what? You will be better for it. You will be better than me. But if you are there because someone told you to go or it was the court's order, you need to really align your heart and desire to get better, or you are just going to push through the emotions. Maybe jump ship while in there, and never change because you were there for all the wrong reasons.

You see, I was in rehab because I wanted to shut everyone up. I wanted everyone to quit telling me I was an addict and needed help. I was there for all the wrong reasons. I thought I was there for me, but in the end, I wasn't. That's why I didn't last. But NOT YOU! I believe you are there for all the right reasons. It is tough, I know! You're not making any money. You are far away from your kids. You miss your family and the birthdays.

You are not sure how things are going to be when you get out. But make sure you are there for all the right reasons and not the wrong ones. This will be the best physical and emotional investment you have ever made in your life. I know you're thinking of walking out. Don't do it. I know you're thinking, *Can I really finish this*? Yes, you can, but you have to really want it. Don't look at this as a setback. Look at it as time invested in yourself to be a better father, mother, husband, wife, brother, sister, son, or daughter. This world needs you, and your family needs you.

But we need the sober, clean version of you. Sadly, this is the first step. You can do this! You might have started life pretty crappy. We let life get the best of us sometimes, don't we? We let addiction take years from us, but when you finish this, you will be better. You will look back and think, *Wow! I really did it*. It's not how you start this life; it's how you finish it! Let's finish it strong!

Much love,
Anthony Torres

LETTER 14

THOUGHTS ABOUT
'MY SASHA'

I'm sitting here in rehab, wondering why you have short conversations with me on the phone. Don't you want to hear from me? This is what you wanted for me. You wanted me to get help. I only get a few moments to hear your voice and the kids'. But as we talk on the phone, I am getting no emotions from you. I wrote you a letter, and you didn't even talk about it. Was I that bad? Have almost nine years of dealing with a drunk and addict made you feel this way towards me? What have several years of talking down to you, lying to you, making you feel like you were nothing done to you? Your heart is so cold and bitter towards me. Was my sorry not enough? You talk to me like a stranger on the phone, not like the father of your kids that I am.

We had some great years together, but I think we can agree that some of those situations were not fair to you or the kids when it got bad. I put all of you in those spots, and I am sorry. You're a strong woman for staying with me all those years, for putting up with me for all those years. I am not sure I would have stuck it out with you if the story was reversed, but you did. Coming home to an empty house after being out all night still hurts me so much. Seeing the kids' rooms empty breaks me deeply as a father; I saw nothing but trash, candy wrappers, and the girls' missed socks on the floor. Caleb's sippy cup full of rotten juice was in the corner; it was probably lost under his bed. But knowing that you had enough of our life together and really decided to leave me. Well, I don't blame you! I would have left sooner.

You fought for our family for so long, but I guess a person can only take so much. How many times would I not come home for days? How many times did I tell you to leave if you didn't like who I was? How many times did you cry and pour your heart out for me to stop? One morning, I remember after being gone all night, drunk, high, and ignoring your calls from the night before, I heard your voice mail. I thought for sure you would cuss me out and tell me what a horrible person I was, but you didn't. With your cracking voice, and I'm sure you had tears running down the side of your face, you said, "Please answer, so I know you're okay at least. Please come home." This broke me inside! This made me weep, knowing how bad I was hurting my family. This upset me, knowing I had spent my night with a bunch of strangers instead of my own family, but I couldn't stop using. I couldn't stop drinking! I just couldn't. Instead of waking up to the mother to my kids, I was waking up next to strangers.

I wanted to stop making a mess of my life, but I didn't know how to. And for all of this, you need to know how truly sorry I am. I hope one day you can forgive me and heal the right way.

Sitting in rehab without you and the kids has gotten to me so much. I am not sure I even know how to process these emotions that I am feeling. And I am doing it sober and falling apart! I have had a headache for three days, my skin is itching, and I can't stop these night sweats. I have been grumpy and angry all day, and I don't know why. The only thing that is keeping me sane is a good cup of coffee and my cigarette breaks. I started to read the Bible. I'm not sure it is helping, but whoever wrote the Psalms seems to be speaking to me. It's deep emotional stuff! I can tell whoever wrote it was broken like me or searching for something like me.

I think about you and the kids every minute of every day. I will do anything to hear your voice getting after me about not helping with the house. I will do anything to see you roll your eyes at me because James was coming over so we could make BBQ and watch our Cowboys play. I will do anything to hear my kids running around the house. I will do anything to hear Harley bark when someone would ring the doorbell. It's crazy how we take the little sounds and the little things for granted in our lives. But here I am! Alone, knowing that everything I had, everything I loved, is gone. I miss you so much! I have cried myself to sleep a few nights like a child holding his blanket. I feel empty, and I feel a hole in my heart. A void I am not sure can ever be filled again.

Out there, you rescued me so many times; it's like I was your child. When I got sick from doing so much drugs and drinking, you would take care of me and feed me. You would make sure I was getting enough water. Some nights at 3 am, I was still up in the garage listening to "Knockin' On Heaven's Door," without you even knowing I just had my last line of cocaine, and processing thoughts of killing myself, feeling so unlovable.

When I would see that door open, I thought for sure you were going to get upset at me, but you would go in the garage, grab my hand and say, "Please come rest." With my tired eyes rolling in the back of my head, slurred speech, and tired voice, I said, "Okay." You still loved me in the mess I was in. I still remember that time I was so sick and throwing up yellow. I had nothing in my stomach to give. I said, "I need to go to the hospital." I had so much pain. You got me by the hand, with

my breath of death and still smelling like a bar. You grabbed
my hand and led me to the shower.

These are the many times you took care of me! The truth is
I took your love for granted. I took your gentle spirit, smile,
touch, and beautiful face for granted. And now you are gone!

As I sit here, I can only think you are seeing someone else.
It just seemed too easy for you to let go. Did you get tired of
fighting for me? And if so, I did that! I pushed you so far away
from me. I left you with no other choice. I just hope that one
day, you will see the good in me like you once did. I hope one
day you can forgive me for taking away almost nine years of
your life that you can never get back. I hope one day you can
heal from all the emotional abuse I put you through, all the
stress and worries I caused you. Be at peace now, love! You're
far away from me now. I can't hurt you and the kids no more.
You don't have to hear my lies anymore and no more broken
promises. I am not sure what my life looks like from here. I am
not sure if I can beat this. I am not sure if this demon I have will
kill me. But I will do my best for the kids. The truth is I don't
even know what to say anymore. Again, I am so sorry!

Your addicted love,
Anthony Torres

LETTER 15

'A LETTER TO MY ANTHONY'
BY SASHA MARIE

A t 5:00am when you were banging on my front door demanding to see our son, I knew we had passed a point of no return. Repeatedly telling you that I wasn't going to open the door until you went to sober up was a new strength I never had before.

I wasn't going to allow you to dictate my life anymore and I didn't even know what that meant. Eight years of the same promises being broken time after time, I knew that I couldn't go back to the same rehearsed lines.

When your mother called me that next morning, I knew that we had lost you. After all the threats, you finally gave in. What would I tell my kids? I was so angry with you. How could you just give up on yourself, on us?!

I waited for a phone call, a text message. Some sign that you were alive and that I was just having crazy, anxious thoughts.

Your mom came over with a cigarette in one hand and her cell phone in the other, in a calm panic. We chatted for a minute. Both wondering what she would find when she got to the house. Your lifeless body, an empty house, or you passed out from a binger. Neither one of us was too sure. But desperately, quietly praying you were alive.

I remember waiting, praying, begging God to just help you. Pacing around my living room as son played with his toys, completely oblivious to what could possibly unfold was torture for me.

My phone rang, my heart stopped, then pounded out of my chest.

"Hello..?"

"He's alive! He was passed out on the floor in his own vomit. He wrecked the house. Smashed in the walls, broke all pictures, smashed the furniture, it's awful in that house. There was beer bottles and baggies everywhere."

Instantly anger set in replacing the hope that you weren't dead. That was our house! The house we were trying to build as a safe place for our children, and YOU WRECKED IT!!

I didn't even have it in me to cry. I just wanted you to go away and get better. I wanted you to stop hurting; me, the kids, yourself.

What was it going to take for you to realize you needed something more than any of us could give you?

And to think, just weeks before your mom called and said they had managed to talk you into rehab. I was happy, but also very much numb. I wanted you to be well for so long and it seemed like it was already too late. So now, I was selfish. Great news for you. You get to go away and get well after ruining all of our lives..? All I could do at that point was wish you well.

Going to see you before you left to rehab that day was rough. I didn't know if I would slap you in the face or talk to you.

Walking in and seeing you sitting there in your mom's surgery scrubs after a 3 day binge was even harder. You were so broken. You seemed so small as you slouched down on that bed. Defeat, fear, guilt, regret all rolled into that crease in your forehead. I felt so helpless. I felt all of your regret. I couldn't help but want to help you again. I just didn't have anything left to give you. What else could I say? What else could I do to show you how much we needed you? How much we loved you? How much we desperately wanted you to be well?

There was nothing else I could do except sit next to you and tell you that I was sorry, sorry that I couldn't do more. I was sorry that I was never enough for you. I was sorry that the kids and I couldn't make you happy. And that I hoped that you would find the help you needed all of those years.

I looked into your eyes, welled up with tears. You looked back at me and with every ounce of strength, which wasn't much, you said you were so sorry. Sorry for not being the man I needed.

Hearing that something broke inside of me. I needed you. I wanted you. I desperately wished that God would change it in that instant. But that was just a fairytale that I made up in my head. It would never be how I wanted it to be. Not as long as you were you. I knew that I had to let you go.

The thought of you going to a Rehabilitation Center made me cringe. How could I protect you in that place? How could I make sure you were ok, that you ate, that you felt safe? Like I did for so long. I was more than the mother of your children, I was your friend, your lover, your peace. It felt like I was sending my child to a cold, dark, and scary place and I couldn't stand it.

As tears fell down my cheeks, you wiped them away and told me not to cry. How could I not?

I lost the battle. I wasn't able to help you. I failed you. My heart was broken again, but for different reasons. I just wanted us to be ok. I wished you would take it all back. I wished you were strong enough to just be better. I wished you could take care of us like you had always promised.

Again, I realized it would never happen.

Looking down at the floor, I told you that I loved you. That I would take care of the kids and that I hoped that you would get better. I wiped the tears from your face and kissed your forehead telling you that I would be there for you no matter what. I would always be your friend. I would do what I could when you got home to make sure you were the best dad you could be. I knew that was all I could do. Promise you that I would be here as your friend when you got out.

Still, putting you first like I had done for so many years. Walking out of that house that day, my heart was broken. I could only pray and hope that you would change.

Sadly, after everything that had happened there was no change. Nothing was enough for you. Not me, not the kids, not even rehab.

As much as it hurts, I have to let you go.

Sasha

"In a time that I should have gone forward, I was going backward. Why was that?"

LETTER 16

THOUGHTS ABOUT
'WHAT WE KNOW VERSUS WHAT WE GO BACK TO'

Isn't it crazy to think that, in recovery, we go back to what we hate? We go back to what we came out of. We go back to that same pain and mess. Back to drugs and alcohol, why is that? It is because we go back to what we know, what we are familiar with. It's almost like we are afraid to be clean and sober, or what that can look like in our lives. It's almost like we feel guilty for wanting to have a good life. We know that we need to get better. We know that some things need to change, but we go back. Do we not think we deserve a good life?

There I was, standing in the doorway of our house. I had been gone for a little over two weeks. It was 8:30 am, and I had just got out of detox/rehab; drunk and high again! I was dropped off at my house after staying in El Paso for a few days. I wasn't home, but somewhere that looked like home. I literally came back to my hell. The electricity was off, and I had letters at the door that they were getting ready to close up the house due to non-payment. Food had been rotting in the fridge for days, and the smell of opened beer cans, rotten food were in the air and left a stench in my nose.

I can't remember if the kids took the turtles or if they died while I was gone. I made holes in the wall by punching them before I left, turned over bookshelves and trashed everywhere. This would be my home for a week. I had no place to go, so I had to stay there in the condition it was in. I didn't know where to turn to. Everyone I loved and needed had turned their backs on me; the support system I had was gone.

I didn't blame them, but I was on my own now. No one to answer to and no one to check up on me. Just me! I used candles at night to keep light in the house. I would go to Mc Donald's to charge my phone for the day. I continued in my addiction. I couldn't go back to work. I felt sick every day, throwing up. I was just waiting for my body to give out. I believe a body can only take so much addiction. The truth is I was afraid. I was alone, and my mind wouldn't shut off. I cried, laughed, and tried to make the best of where I was at. But one day, I couldn't stay in that house anymore. It was like a movie that would play in my mind. I would see my kids running around the house and Sasha cooking us dinner.

I could remember all the fights we had in the living room, all the memories that were now lost in the wind. I wasn't getting better staying in that home, so I needed to leave. I left, and that night, I slept on a bench in the park. That was the worst feeling in the world! Would I now be homeless? I am thankful that was my last night outside as I had my club brothers and my cousin put me up on their sofas for different nights. If it wasn't for them, I would have been on the streets. I tell people all the time that I should have died in that home.

Have you ever been afraid to die alone? It's the worst feeling in the world. Dying as you're lost in your thoughts. Dying with nobody around. Dying an addict. I didn't know what to do with my life. In that moment, I was lost. I was searching for something! I couldn't stand the sight of myself in the mirror.

But I knew what I needed to do; I needed to get better. Were all rehabs like the one I experienced? One night out at a bar, I sat on my motorcycle, lit a cigarette, looked up in the sky, and began to curse the so-called God for creating me. If this is all my life was, I didn't want it. Why was I here? Why was I born? Why was this happening? And, of course, I got no answer; he seemed to be silent when I needed an answer.

The life that I once knew was gone, but it's like I was okay with it in that moment. With all my why(s) and questions, it was a spot I got myself into, and I had to be okay with it. I missed my kids but I'm not sure what I thought about Sasha. I was angry with her, purely frustrated! Word on the street was that she was with someone else, and the thought of that tore me up inside. I had a rubber band of rage that was bouncing around inside of me. I needed to get out of this city. I didn't want to stay, and I was afraid I would do something that I would regret. I was not right in my mind. There was a fire upstairs in my mind, and I didn't know how to put it out.

Most of the time I was in Cruces, I stayed high every day. I didn't like to come down. I ate when I needed to. I stayed up for days till my body gave up, and I slept. I even smiled when I could. I was just a roaming drunk with no direction. The bars would become my home.

One morning after waking up at my cousin's house, he told me how I smelled so bad because I hadn't showered in days. "Shower!" he said. In a time that I should have gone forward, I was going backward. Why was that?

Because this is what I was okay with! We don't go to what we don't know. We go back to what makes us feel good. An addict is more afraid of the unknown than anything. We are afraid to see past our addictions, and we feel we don't deserve to have a good life. It is the wrong way to think! We do deserve a good life.

Listen, you deserve a great life. I know you don't think so right now. How many times have I heard people ask me, "Why do you keep going back?" It is because it is what we know, friend. It's what we are okay with. It's what we do. You can't be afraid to walk in the unknown. You can't be afraid to try new things and experience a new journey.

Today, I am here to tell you that you shouldn't apologize to anyone for wanting to be happy in life. Right now, I know your addiction probably has you stuck. It's probably been years, but you can get out of this runt. I asked myself why I kept going back, and the answer was simple; either we go back to what we know, or we muster up strength and courage to change and get our life right. Get back what we lost, get ourselves out of this hole we created.

Remember, it's that safe place that we created for ourselves, and guess what? We have to create a new safe place for us, but it will all start by changing our thinking. I don't want to spend too much time on this point in this letter because I want to talk about it in another letter. If there are any words that I can leave you in this thought, read the next paragraph.

I might have described your life now; just a roaming drunk or addict with no sense of direction. You know what happens when we just roam, right? You know we don't just get lost, but eventually, we will hit a wall. Have you hit that wall yet? Put your hand over your heart. Do you feel that? It's called life; as long as you have the heartbeat, it's another day to make things right. I wasted my days trying to get better. I don't want you to do the same.

Thanks for letting me share my heart with you on this one.

Much love,
Anthony Torres

"As long as you know you did everything to make amends, let God handle the rest. Let him heal those hearts. Let him give people the strength to forgive"

LETTER 17

THOUGHTS ABOUT
'MY KIDS'

Have you ever rode on a Greyhound bus? It's seriously one of the longest drives ever! I mean, why do they have to stop at every single gas station they see? It probably was a good 24 hours since I last had one sip of alcohol or drugs in my system. I was literally cracking inside. I was itching within my own skin to get high or get a drink. It was like I could feel my body going through shock and withdrawal. But here I was, stuck on this bus back to Oklahoma because my mother felt I needed to get out of New Mexico due to my state of mind and with everything going on.

She wasn't wrong. So here I was, on this long road of no-where—this long road to uncertainty. This road that I had created. I will say this; being on a Greyhound bus really makes you think. I tried my best to collect my thoughts on that long drive on the road, and there are some things beautiful in the state of New Mexico. The sunsets and thunderstorms are amazing, and desert rain has its own scent. As the rain began to fall on the window and the sound of cracking thunder coming from outside, a mind could wonder about those who had nowhere to go, but I believe it gets deeper being sober and clean. It's like we get to see what we have become. We get to see what we have turned into. For once, while sitting on that bus and with nothing to do, I started to do some deep thinking. My spirit was calm, and my mind was on alert.

I missed my kids, my life, and my routine. Just like that, my life was changed and altered. It was there and now gone like a paper burning in the fire, nothing but ashes. I was on this bus with literally no money and barely any clothes. But I learned something that day. I learned that material things could be replaced, but not family. Here I was, on a bus, smelling like cigarettes and unwashed armpits. It was probably a couple of days since I had showered. My cousin did remind me that I stank, remember? HA!

Sometimes when I would be high and think about my life, I would put on a CD by Seether, Stone Sour, or Stained. I can say this, Shaun Morgan, Corey Taylor, and Aaron Lewis got me through some of the darkest times in my life. I would hear the lyrics to these men's songs. In one of Shaun's songs, he said, "It seems like every day is the same, and I'm left to discover on my own. It seems like everything is grey, and there's no color to behold. They say it's over, and I'm fine again. Yeah, try to stay sober; feels like I'm dying here" I would hear these words and think if these guys could get through life in their darkest moments, so could I! If these guys could make it, so can I! Even though I will never meet these men, I was thankful for their music that got me through the lowest moments in my life. Maybe you can relate to some songs that got you by as well. Music speaks to the hidden areas of our hearts. Those areas that no one knows about.

Your mind is a deep and terrible place. Sometimes it takes you to places you don't want to go to; it entertains thoughts you wish you never processed. The mind is a deep ocean no man has ever discovered before; it's a deep, dark, scary, and sometimes lonely place. The deeper we go, the more we think. This is how I felt on this bus; my mind wouldn't shut off!

I thought I was never going to see my kids again. The hardest part for me as a father was telling my kids I was sick and that I needed to go away for a while.

One day, Sasha brought them to see me before I went away to detox. As I got off my bike, Bella and Ili came running to me with joy to see their dad. Caleb was too small to run, so Sasha put him in my arms. And with a broken, tired voice, I said, "I have to go away for a while." With their gentle voices, they asked, "Why?" They didn't understand, but I could still see their faces were crushed. Their spirits and smiles were also crushed. I remember hugging all three of them, and one of the kids asked me, "Daddy, where are you going?" And all I could say was that I was going away to get better. Tears began to roll down their eyes, my lip quivered, and tears began to roll down my eyes too. Having all three of their little arms hugging me so tight would be something I would never forget. I hurt my kids, and I was not okay with that. It broke me! I would see them again one day. Would I? I haven't seen my other daughter in months.

My three little girls had been through enough of my broken promises, enough of my crap, enough of me playing dad sometimes. One time, my girls had a soccer game, and there I was, hungover, laying on the ground with a pounding headache, acting like I was paying attention. As I clapped and cheered them on, I was sick inside, and they never knew.

My kids had been through enough of my late-night parties at home. They had been through enough of me being drunk on Halloween. They had been through enough of me being drunk on Thanksgiving. Why did I have to be drunk at every single birthday party that you guys had? Why could I not just let you enjoy your day? And I always had to make it about me, my loves! It was enough, and it was time for me to get better.

With pain in my weak knees and heart, I gave Caleb back to Sasha, let go of the girls' little hands, and walked away. Looking at the girls and Caleb and turning away was the hardest thing I have ever done. I hope they knew how much that hurt me. I hope they knew how much I love them. I hope they understood the pain in my heart when I was about to leave them. I didn't want to! But it was either I got better somehow or have my kids bury me and grow up without a dad. Kids are so innocent and loving. They don't care what has been done sometimes; they just want their parents. They want the love of their mother and father.

I love you, Bella, Iliana, Angelina, Caleb. I hope you all have forgiven me.

Caleb, you were too small to know or see anything. My prayer is that you would be a better young man than I was. I pray you never have to go through dark and tough times like I did, son. Even at your age, you're a better version of me. I love you!

Girls, I hope you forgive me for making mom cry. Forgive me for all the late nights you heard me and mom screaming and cussing at each other. Forgive me for always drinking early in the morning. Forgive me for throwing up because I was hungover and sick from drugs all night, and all Bella and sometimes, Ili, could say was, "Dad, are you okay?"

Forgive me for putting you in harm's way by drunk driving with you guys in the car. Forgive me for getting my drugs with you in the car while you were in the presence of those drug dealers as we exchanged hands.

Forgive me, daughters and son! I am sorry that I had people over at the house for late-night drinking, especially strangers you never met, and we partied all night while you fell asleep on the couch without blankets.

I am sorry you had to go through times of confused thoughts. I am sorry for ripping you guys from your home, and you now live at grandma's due to my actions. I am sorry you had to leave your rooms at home. I am sorry I broke up our home and family; I am sorry! I am sorry that I chose to get high and drink all night instead of spending time with you watching movies.

I am sorry! Please forgive me. God knows I have made my share of mistakes as a father and as a man. I don't know where I went wrong, kids. I don't know how I let something that started out so small get out of control in my life. I don't know where I lost myself. I'm sorry that I dragged you into this; it was not fair to you.

Caleb, son, I thought having you would help me to get better. I thought having my boy would finally help me sober up and get clean, but it didn't. Momma would probably say it got worse.

You guys need to know those four months apart from you were so hard for me, not waking up to hearing your sweet voices. Oh, I missed this so much. I understand I can never get this time back with you, neither can I take the pain and confusion I have caused in your life, but I hope one day, you will understand that we all make mistakes. This one was mine, and I am sorry. I hope one day you can forgive me.

These were all the thoughts I had on the bus; all I could do was think. My mind was taking me back to regret, shame, guilt, and the thought of being a failure! I know you're thinking, *Wow! You just let it all out.* I think honesty is everything when it comes to our kids, and it's also good for us in recovery. Because sometimes it's hard to move forward and heal from areas of our lives if we don't confess, own up to our mistakes and heal from them in time. You have so much time to process your life and process your thoughts when you are on a long journey on a bus. Someday, I was hoping I would be able to make it up to them. In my heart, I was hoping they could forgive me someday.

I don't know where your kids are now, maybe with your spouse, grandparents, parents, or the state. But I know what you're thinking. *Will they ever forgive me? Will they ever let me be apart of their life again? Can I make it up to them?* And the answer is YES, but you must remember it will not be on your time; it will be on theirs. I don't want you to give up and go back to drugs just because your kids don't want anything to do with you. Don't go back to drugs because things are not going how you had thought. It takes time. You might be saying you don't have time. As long as you know you did everything to make amends, let God handle the rest. Let him heal those hearts. Let him give people the strength to forgive. You did your part in asking for forgiveness and confessing your mistakes; let him do his part. I know you want those birthday parties back. You want back those moments of hearing their voices over the phone. You want back that one kiss and embrace. Give it time!

My daughters are now 21,20,18, and Caleb is 12, and where has the time gone. But my girls have had their dad sober and clean for 11 years. It wasn't easy, but I believe our relationships have slowly healed in some areas. They said they had forgiven me, and I believe that.

I can say this, no matter how distant you are from your kids, they know you love them. They know you care. No matter how much pain you think you caused them, they will heal. I just need you to stay focused, regardless of where you are. Stay on this journey of getting sober and clean. I believe in you. Thanks for letting me share my thoughts with you. On to the next one.

Much love,
Anthony Torres

"What's been cut will heal! So will

your kids, and so will you"

LETTER 18

THOUGHTS ABOUT
'PTSD CHILD'

I have once said that addiction affects everyone and everything it touches. The ripple effect it has is damaging and
even as people grow and heal in their lives. Some things
can happen to make them remember about a time they're trying to forget about. I believe it can be even more felt with our
own kids, with the things they saw while growing up.

Not sure if I still have it, but Sasha once took a picture of
Iliana when she was smaller, looking out the window door as
I was leaving after Sasha and I had just gotten into a heated
argument back in the day. As I jumped on my bike and glanced
at the house, I could see her little face was pressed up against
the glass with her juice cup in her left hand and her pigtails
crooked from laying down on the couch. I could see she was
crying, and I will never get her little beautiful brown eyes out
of my head. She was confused again.

Maybe because I would endlessly leave the house to go out
for the night, and I would pick her up her in my arms and tell
her, "*Mija,* don't worry, I will be right back," and the truth is I
never came back. I only returned days after the urge to use
drugs and drink got out of my system. At that age, she already
knew that she would not see me for a few days. She never liked
it when I would leave

If my kids could write a book, they probably would? I think they were pretty taken care of in their young years. They had everything they needed. We moved a lot, but other than that, you look at pictures of them when they were small, and they lacked nothing. I can say I worked hard to provide for them, but growing up in a home where dad was a drunk can affect any child. From strangers in the home to late-night parties to being at a friend's house late because I didn't want to leave yet. Sasha would often get so angry with me and leave me there; sometimes I went home, and sometimes, I didn't. But what she didn't know earlier on was that I was high on coke most of the time, and I didn't want my high to go away, so I was waiting for more. That probably caused more fights for Sasha and me during those days. I can count more problems for us as a family.

But our fights were ugly when they did happen, like Mike Tyson and Sugar Ray ugly. I never hit her, but we would get into many shouting matches, and we called each other every name you can think of in the cussing dictionary. Sometimes we would push each other, backed up with "I'm calling the cops." If my memory serves me right, I think the cops were only called one time. Most of the time, she started the fights by stopping me from leaving because I wanted to get drunk and high. Sometimes we would turn things up a bit, throw stuff at each other, or start throwing clothes out the door. Sometimes I would throw my beer can at her because she made me so mad for nagging at me! What an awful human I was. Sometimes she would hit me in the face with whatever she could find. And then there were kids, right in the middle of all that drama, hearing every word and seeing everything with their innocent eyes.

I don't know how many times Sasha would cruise the city looking for me with the kids in the back of the car, wondering where I was; from bar to bar, house to house, hotel to hotel, wondering who I was with or what I was doing. She did that for some time, and then after a while, she just stopped looking for me. Sometimes, even our loved ones get tired of fighting.

After a while, I would ride my motorcycle to El Paso just to get away from the search for me. Can you imagine me on the highway going 75 mph - 80 mph, drunk and high with no helmet? I did that often and wondered why I was still alive. I still remember those nights and wonder how I got home. I often saw my motorcycle on its side in the driveway; I probably spent many nights crawling inside the house.

With all my heart, I believe Iliana does have PTSD from all the things she saw or heard while growing up, and it was proven to me the other night. Bella and Angie may not be as vocal as their little sister. Caleb wasn't born till later, so he was too small to remember anything.

One night, Sasha and I had a disagreement (yes, Christian marriages still have disagreements from time to time), but I am happy to say our disagreements are way different from ten years ago; nothing is thrown, and we both know tomorrow is a new day.

But now, when we have disagreements, I go to the church to work instead of going out to the bars. The church is my safe place! It was 12:20 am, and my phone chimed with a text alert that read, "Dad, when are you coming home? Are you okay?" I replied with, "Soon, I am almost done." She then texted, "Okay, I love you," and I replied, "I love you too, honey."

At 1:30 am, Ili texted again, "Daddy, you're not home yet," I answered, "Will be soon, baby (sending her a pic of my desk and me working). Go to bed, sweetie. It's late." Illi then replied, "I can't."

At 2 am, I walked through the door and heard a click of her light being turned off. She could sleep now because daddy was home. It's been ten years, and I believe Iliana suffers from what I put her through as a child. It's like a scene that plays over and over again in her head. All she hears is, "I will be home soon." It takes her back when she would hear those words, and I never returned. The Roaring lion of PTSD starts to play out in her mind.

I wonder; I just wonder as it got me thinking. If she was 17 when I was an addict, would she still wait up for me to come home? Would she say, "Are you okay, daddy?" And I wonder if her sweet voice on the phone, a text, or GiF from her would bring me back home. I wonder if I would still be an addict and out of control, roaming the streets and hopping from bar to bar. Would her love for me be enough?

The past is the past; we can't change that. We can only change the now. But I believe what we can do is allow our children to healthily heal on their own time. We should allow our children to vent to us about how they feel or how we made them feel and recognize it for what it is. It is something that has scared them. I don't want you to start getting down on yourself; we can't change that. But we can work on today and tomorrow with our children. Help be a part of the healing process in their lives. Will you do me a favor? Allow yourself to heal too. I have been there before, and what does that look like? It always starts with asking those you hurt for forgiveness.

I will end with this; what's been cut will heal! So will your kids, and so will you. Let's look forward to brighter days and new memories with our family. Remember, it's not how you start, it's how you finish! Finish strong, my friend.

Much love,
Anthony Torres

"We have all been to a place of

darkness when it comes to suicide,

but the truth is we need you!"

LETTER 19

Thoughts about
'When the Voices Don't Stop'
(My Suicidal Note)

Whenever I hear of someone committing suicide, my heart literally drops! I feel my spirit crumble inside. The joy in me zaps out. Why? Because I have been in that spot before. A place of darkness, a place we are not sure we can come out of. It's like a movie I watched a while back; this SEAL team went into a village. There were bombs, missiles from planes, and the enemies shooting at them from every angle, but they had to go in the war, and sadly some didn't make it out. This reminds me of those that are suicidal. They are in this place and stuck between staying and speaking out.

A place where that enemy shoots at their thoughts of "you're worthless." And the whispers of the devil that "the pain is too much for you, just die." "They will be fine without you; nobody will miss you." It's in that moment that we wrestle in our own minds; *Should I gamble with the afterlife?* Sadly, some come out, and some don't. I never understood suicide until I heard the voices when I was 24, and I started to feel the heaviness to the extent that I couldn't shake. It seemed the voices and darkness got more intense when I entered rehab, and I was at my lowest. But they got louder when I got off that bus in Oklahoma.

So I sat there, and this was it. I had enough, not to get better, but to die. So I began to plan:

I'm sorry that it really got to this point in time in my life, but it has. I must end my life. I'm tired! Just tired! Tired of the failures. Tired of the ups and downs of life. Tired of letting people down. I don't think I can ever stop doing drugs. I really don't think I can ever stop drinking. It has become a part of me, but it has gotten worse! My body is tired; it hurts! It's weak. It's like forcing myself to get up and get going throughout my day. Putting this mask on that everything is okay in my life is more tiring than just facing the reality of what is going on inside of me. I'm trying to make people think I am really okay, but I'm hurting and not okay deep down inside.

I miss my grandpa and grandma. I think about them daily! Is there an afterlife? I hope so. I think anything will be better than this. But the voices! They won't stop. They are telling me to end my life. They are telling me how worthless I am. They are telling me things I don't want to hear. Have you ever heard a fork scrape up against a plate? That high pitch sound, that's how the voices sound. My eyes are shut tight. I have my hands over my ears. I am screaming, but nothing is coming out! Are the voices lying to me? Nobody cares about me, and the truth is nobody will miss me when I am gone. I am the problem. So the problem will be solved! I can hear the voices getting louder. Stop it! Get out of my head! Leave me alone!

You will find me dead, you'll be shocked when you get the phone call, and you might say, "Maybe we should have listened to him more," "I can't believe he did this." Regrets will set in. "I should have called him more," "Was I really there for him?" You will cry on the day I die. You will grieve during my burial, and I am sorry that I had to put you through this. But then, after that, your life will go on. As the years go on, I will just be a memory of your thoughts, and you will live your life.

You will meet someone else, and again I will just be that memory in your thoughts. There will be "RIP" on my Facebook, and everyone will comment "Rest in Peace," but I didn't die in peace. I died with pain, a pain no one will ever know about.

The only regret I will have in doing this is my children. My pain will now become theirs, and they will never understand why I did it. Will this become permanent pain in their own life? They will hurt knowing that there was nothing they could do to stop their daddy from doing this. Sadly, their life will be altered forever. I hope they won't need counseling in their lives.

Nobody will ever understand why I did it. I'm sure people will say I was weak, I was looking for the easy way out, I was a coward, or maybe I was just looking for attention. And they can say what they want. But nobody will ever understand my emotional pain or my state of mind. Those voices will just not shut up! The heaviness just got the best of me, and those demons won.

People always judge what they don't understand.

How would I do it? I tried many times to bring the gun to my head and couldn't pull the trigger. I can't hang myself. I don't think I could do this to my aunt and uncle, finding my lifeless body with a rope around my neck, giving them that picture that will forever be in their heads.

I have a plan! When I would get back from being out all night, I would find a way. Even if it meant overdosing on pills, heroin, I would find a way somehow. This was my last night here. So I sent a text out to get what I needed to end my life. I bought pills to kill myself.

It was that night at the bar. With every drink, I thought, and with every cigarette smoke puffed, I cried. I thought about my children. I thought about what my life had become. With every snort of cocaine in the bathroom stalls, I hurt and bled inside. I remember telling a girl I was dancing with that, "This will be my last night here." She laughed, of course, because we lived in a military city. I'm sure she thought I was getting ready to ship out across the seas.

Shot after shot, I was ready to end my life. I had built so much Dutch courage. My whole body was numb, and my mind didn't care. All I remember was that girl asking me to dance again, and I believe that last dance probably saved me.

This was the only night that I was thankful for alcohol because I drank so much that I blacked out! When I was ready to die, my addiction didn't allow me to. Not even knowing what house I was at, just here lying next to 'I like to call her'-One last dance- It was morning, and the sun rays were getting through the crease of the curtain and hitting my damp face. I tried to slowly open my eyes, but eye boogers were keeping them shut. With a dry cough and vomit on my pants, I got up, went to the sink, and washed my face. With my bloodshot eyes, I looked at myself in the mirror, and I coughed and began to gag with phlegm coming out. Spitting this junk out of my lungs as they hurt, my whole body was hurting. My mind wouldn't shut off! Something needed to change in my life, or next time, I wasn't going to wake up.

I really believe you're not just reading this book by accident; you're reading it for a purpose. I'm not sure how you got it, but it's in your hands. Remember how I shared with you in one thought that things were starting to get my attention that I needed to change some things in my life. If you're reading this now, you need to come out of that war zone! Don't go back in. Don't walk! I need you to start running because I am afraid that when you come out, you might go right back into the war on drugs or alcohol in your life. And this time, you just might not come out if you go back in. Remember what I told you! You have the shovel; stop digging yourself deeper.

I am not sure how I got out. I am not sure how I made it, but I did, and the pain I had in my heart caused me to write this. People I know or counseled didn't make it out, but you can! It's another day to make things right with yourself and those around you. I wrote this thought because I want you to know that you're not alone in this battle; there are people like you and me who can also come out of it. This is something you never have to be ashamed of, friend. Don't be embarrassed to admit your emotional or mental state. We have all been to a place of darkness when it comes to suicide, but the truth is we need you!

I want you to overcome this. I blacked out for a reason, and it was to write this book. It was to communicate a message of hope and tell you that "You can make it," "You can overcome." You just have to believe in yourself. I really should not be here today, but by God's grace, I am.

I said in the beginning that Sasha would move on If I had committed suicide, and I believe she would have. That pain would be with her, but she would live again. The pain would be passed down to my kids, and it probably would have affected them for the rest of their lives. I could never imagine what their thought process would be, growing up without a dad who killed himself.

I want to end with this. I don't know what emotional state you are in right now, and I don't know how much you're telling yourself to hang to another day. You're probably saying, "Will this pain ever stop?" It can, and it will. One day, the hurt will stop. You have to believe that the storms at the seas will calm one day. You don't see it now, but they will. Please hang on! I can't wait to share my next thought with you. I hope it will inspire you somehow.

Much love,
Anthony Torres

"I don't want to lose my dad.

You are hurting your health and

your family. Jesus can save you.

Why are you so angry?"

LETTER 20

'A LETTER TO MY DAD'
BY ILIANA TORRES

Dear Dad,

I want you to know I love you, but I wish you were here with your family. I'm old enough to notice when you're gone. My heart hurts to hear mom cry herself to sleep. I don't understand why you hurt her; she loves you, and all she wants is a father to love her kids. She is always there for you. Why aren't you protecting her? I thought you loved us. Do you love your addiction more than your family? Family is supposed to be there for each other, care, protect, cherish, love, and understand one another, and be a safe place.

Grandma has been taking me to church, and there is someone named Jesus, and He loves you and us. I believe you will come back to us, and I hope it is soon. I want a dad. Grandpa has been more of a dad than you have ever been to your own kids. Don't you want me? Did I do something wrong? I just want my dad back. Please come back. All we do is love you. Why can't you see how hurt we are? Open your eyes, please! Why can't you just open your eyes and see what you're doing?

I don't want to lose my dad. You are hurting your health and your family. Jesus can save you. Why are you so angry? We lost everything because you are more in love with your drugs and alcohol than trying to get your family back. I just don't understand. Every-one keeps telling me to stop crying about the little things, but I don't take the time to ask what the big things hurting me are, making the little ones hurt more than they should. I just want my dad back. We stay up all night, eating and walking around to find something to do to pass the time. We are learning how to survive without you. I don't want to be without you, but you don't want us. How am I supposed to love a man? I just have so many questions. I pray you find the answers, and I don't want to lose my daddy to drugs. Please come home

Love,
Your daughter,
Iliana.

"My soul was not lost but found.

My heart was no longer empty but

full"

LETTER 21

THOUGHTS ABOUT
'FALSE GOD'

We always hear the term "hardened heart". What does that really mean? It can probably mean a lot of things, depending on the person or situation. Being stubborn and prideful can play a huge part in that. Over the years, I have seen the meanest, worst, tattooed men and women turn their lives around. People would look at them, judge them, and say, "There is NO hope for them." I wonder if people said the same thing about me. But seeing them live a clean and sober life brings me immense joy. I know it was not always like that for them. They say many people have to hit rock bottom for their hearts to be softened or before they can see the truth. What is our rock bottom? What is our lowest? I believe it can be different for anyone. I know people who have been in and out of jail multiple times; they are down to nothing and still find the urge to use drugs again. Wanting to change has to come from the heart, but I believe a hardened heart can make it harder, a heart that is dark and blind to the reality that people can have a great life being sober and clean. A heart that only sees their addiction and the lie for what it is.

I don't want to say that I was an atheist, but I was leaning more towards agnosticism. I had a lot of questions for God. If He was all-powerful, why didn't He stop that drunk driver from hitting my grandparents and killing them instantly? Why didn't He stop my parents from getting a divorce or protect my mother in times of hardship? Why? Why were innocent people suffering? I came from a Catholic Church, but I never got any answers to my questions. I'm sure things were probably explained to me, but I didn't listen. Nothing spoke to my heart.

So I got my own view on who God was and how He worked. Growing up, I became my own God and made my own decisions. I created my own path. I just lived my life and dealt with whatever came and really had no sense of God (spiritually). Besides that, Bible was a history lesson, and it wasn't for today as far as I was concerned. I would cringe at anyone coming at me with a Bible, telling me I needed to go to church or that I needed Jesus. I think there was a time I told a Christian, "YOU NEED JESUS! Leave me alone and worry about your own life (Probably not in those nice words, but you get the picture)"

I would even mock Sasha when she wanted to talk about God or when she said, "God bless." At the breakfast table, when I read an article in the paper about a disaster or someone like an innocent kid dying, I would say things such as, "Look at your God killing innocent babies." I was okay with my hardened heart. I was okay with my own demons. I was okay with my view on life and who God was.

I remember when I wanted to get tattoos, I always wanted to get evil things on my body, such as skulls, demon girls, the devil, and so on. I was the devil's masterpiece, and I was okay with that. If I couldn't be good, I would just be bad and good at it. One time, I stumbled across a Satanic bible and even began to read some of the materials they had to say. When I said I was flirting with darkness, I was really all in! All in with my drugs. All in with my drinking. All in with me being hateful and not caring for this world. I was that guy.

We come across these scary movies about darkness, exorcism, demons, and so on. Brush it off; it's not real. I am here to tell you that darkness is real, and demons are real. The doors that we open are real. I look back at my life and realize how dumb and blind I was. I realize how hardened my heart had gotten over the years. I formed a hateful and judgmental attitude even towards people who went to church.

The truth is that church scared me! Many people go to church on Sundays, acting one way, but they behave differently on Mondays like they never spent time with God. They threw their scriptures around but couldn't even live up to them themselves. Church people showed no grace, mercy, or forgiveness to no one but loved to beg for it on Sundays for themselves. They looked down on me anyway. I would never fit into their culture. I would never fit into a church circle. I was an outcast while growing up, and I would be an outcast then. I would just be a tattooed Hispanic. They would belittle me and throw stones at me. They wouldn't accept me or respect me If I decided to show my face out of curiosity.

So I stayed away. I stayed away from church people. I mocked and cursed God. I would talk down to Sasha when she would try to mention God. "No thanks, you can have your false God! You can keep your Jesus." My heart was so far away from God that even if he was speaking to me, I wasn't listening, or I didn't want to.

As far as I was concerned, there was no God that could help me. He could never forgive me for all the bad I had done in life. He could never heal my heart that had been hurting my whole life. He could never love me because I didn't even love myself. Besides, I had done so much bad In my life that I did not deserve a good life. As long as my kids were okay, I really didn't care what happened to me or how my life turned out. We all have to die one day, and if it was in darkness, so be it. If it meant not believing in God and going to hell, I was okay with it. Hell seemed better than this life anyway.

You're probably wondering what happened to me after the last thought. I left you with me waking up in an unknown house, with me planning suicide, but it never happened. That morning In Oklahoma, I called my aunt to come and get me because I needed a ride back home. She had told me they were going to church and all I could do was roll my eyes like I really didn't want to go. "I am not a church person," I said to her, but she insisted that I go. She said, "You will like Pastor Lopez." I said, "I smell like smoke and like I just jumped out of a beer bottle." She then said, "You will be fine." So I got up, got a napkin, and cleaned the vomit from my pants. And here I was, going to church and having a fit like a kid not getting his way in the toy aisle at Walmart.

What in the world was I thinking? I didn't even like church; I hated church. But it was like something was tugging at my heart to go. Why was I feeling this way? So I went. It couldn't hurt really at this point. What did I have to lose? As I was walking out the door, I just kept telling myself a few things. The first is that Momma would have a fit seeing how I was dressed and how I smelt going to church. Secondly, I hope the church doesn't burn down because I am coming.

August 30th, 2009, I walked into a church, and it is a day I will never forget. Upon entering the church, everyone was staring at me; it was like needles poking me on the side of my cheek. I felt ashamed and embarrassed. *Why was everyone so happy to be at church? Don't they know Sundays are for football?* I sat down and began to stare around and look at everyone. I felt like I was in a foreign land.

The music began to play, and the people were clapping, raising their hands, and shouting to God. The only thing I could think of was that these people are nuts, and they have literally lost their minds. For me, it was too loud in that church. *Why do these people seem so happy singing? They need to be quie*t, I thought. I felt like telling everyone *SHHHHHHHHH!*

After that awful singing time, the Pastor began to speak, and he talked about a guy named Jesus like I never heard before in my entire life. I mean, I should have known this! I carried Jesus on the cross when I was in the Catholic church down the aisle when I was an altar boy. With every word he spoke, it was like he was describing my life to the congregation. Did someone tell this Pastor about what was going on in my life? Did my aunt set me up? What was going on? At that moment, I felt like getting up and walking out, but I waited as my face became hot and numb with every word he spoke. I felt so uneasy within my spirit. And the more I listened to him speak about the character, power, and heart of Jesus; tears began to fall down my face and onto my dirty shirt. I looked down at the dried vomit on my pants and began to think how messed up my life really was. I begin to wipe my eyes because I couldn't cry! I was too tough for this. I was this bad biker dude. Guys with tattoos don't cry, but the tears just began to run down my face, and there was no way of shutting them off,

Then the Pastor said something I had never heard before. "Does someone need prayer? Do you need salvation? If so, come up here, and we can pray with you." *What is this new life he was talking about? Doesn't this Pastor know my past? Doesn't he know that I tried to kill myself last night?* I thought. My aunt then got my hand to walk me up, and I slowly hesitated because I couldn't go up and pray to someone I didn't fully believe in. So with heavy feet like bricks were tied around my ankles, I went up with her. That was the longest walk I ever had to do. I call it the walk of DEFEAT! For once in my life, I was fully defeated as a man. For once, I admitted in my own heart, not trying to mask it my whole life, that I needed something better in my life.

As I looked at the Pastor in the eyes, he asked me, "What can I pray with you about?" I replied, "I don't know. I just got out of rehab, and I am an addict. My family left me." He then asked, "Have you accepted Jesus into your life?" I said, "No, am I supposed to?"

On that day, my heart was open and softened for the first time, and I knew there was something more than what I was feeling or going through in life. And with a small whisper coupled with a cracked, broken, and desperate voice, I said, "Jesus, I need you. I need you to come into my life." Then something spiritual happened to me. It was an experience that I fully can't explain even if I wanted to. Even to this day, I have no words to qualify it.

I can explain that I felt loved in my life like never before; it was different from our parents' kind of love or one that goes away. It's not the love that people only show when things are going their way. But a deep warmth of an embrace of God's eternal love. I felt forgiven. I felt accepted. I felt His grace and mercy towards my life. I believe in my heart that I just had a spiritual experience with Jesus; it's called salvation. My soul was not lost but found. My heart was no longer empty but full. Things in my life were no longer black and white, but I could see things in color. I had a sense of purpose and a sense of value in life, all in 5 seconds. Have you ever had a moment in life and think, *WOW! Where has this been my whole life?* That was the moment for me, and in a good way, I said, "What in the world just happened?"

While reading the Bible and learning more about what happened in my life, I got an itch like never before. It sounds crazy, I know. I felt different. I was thinking differently. I needed to find out what was going on inside of me. I was sure I would find out what was going on sooner or later, but I wanted to share what had happened to me with people. I called my mom and everyone I knew. I was shouting it on social media.

How could I go from wanting to end my life to now finding my life again? How could I go from waking up without a purpose to finding purpose again?

I remembered calling Sasha with tears in my eyes and a big grin on my face. I was smiling so much that my face was hurting, and I said to her, "I know you are upset at me, and I know you wanted me to get better. But I just gave my heart to Jesus." With a long pause, she said, "OOOOOKAAAYYYY. Whatever. Good for you! When are you going to come home and see your kids? They need you."

The truth is she didn't believe me one bit, not even if I told her I wanted to become a priest. She was in that season in her life where nothing I said mattered. She was not going to believe anything that came out of my mouth, and I really couldn't blame her. I couldn't believe what I was saying. I couldn't believe what I was feeling inside my heart.

This was just the beginning of my story; this was just the beginning of my new life. I wish I could say my addictions would go away overnight or that I would be a better person in the morning. I had a lot of work to do. I had a lot of thoughts to process. My journey was now starting. I just wonder how it would all work out or what my life would now be. Thanks for letting me share my experience with you! Thanks for letting me share my heart! Let's get ready for the next thought.

Much love,
Anthony Torres

"I want you to be strong, grow in your faith, and know why you do what you do in your recovery and who you do it for."

LETTER 22

THOUGHTS ABOUT
'WOULD THE CATHOLIC CHURCH DISOWN ME?'

B efore people get upset at me about the title of this thought, understand there is a reason for it. Moving forward, your support group is everything in recovery! And let me make this very clear, I have so much respect for the Catholic Church. I was an altar boy for three years and made my first Holy Communion. I have some great friends who still go to the Catholic Church. Today, can you find support in a Catholic Church? Absolutely! But words and actions of others can be damaging to our hearts in recovery or any situation. You might be wondering what that means.

What I mean is, when you start your journey to recovery, don't crumble if your support group does not support you or if you get shunned by that church you were once a part of.

One time, I had an appointment with an ophthalmologist, and when he was getting my eyes checked, I said, "I can't wait to get my eyes again. I need to see people; everyone is blurry when I speak." He then asked, "What do you do?" I replied, "I pastor a church here in Alamogordo." With Joy in my heart, I shared my story with him about what God has done in my life and still doing. He really didn't care too much that I was clean and sober for so many years. He was more interested in why I was no longer in the Catholic Church. With disappointment in his tone, he asked, "Why did you leave the true Church of Christ (the Catholic Church)?"

In a nutshell, what he was trying to tell me in a very nice way was that I was going to hell, and what I experienced in that other church was not real and was not of God.

Of course, I left that Doctor's office, not feeling discouraged but more focused! If that was me within my first year in recovery, maybe I would have felt a little different. You are probably wondering what I said to him. What I said in a very calm voice was, "Sorry you feel that way, but a building doesn't save people; Jesus does."

In 2009, after giving my heart to Christ in the Church named "Healing Waters," I cried my eyes out, asking Christ to forgive me for cussing at him and doubting him. Later on that day, I remember having a conversation with my mom. Her words were very encouraging. I was not too sure about what she was going to say because we were raised as Catholics. I explained everything that had happened, and she said, *Mijo*, I am so proud of you. I also had a spiritual experience in a church before. Be with God now, *Mijo*, and let Him guide your path." Hearing my mom speak these words was so comforting to me in my newfound journey.

You are probably wondering why I mentioned this in this book. It is because most Hispanics are raised Catholics. You don't know how many conversations I have had with men and women in recovery whose families disowned because they attended church or program that was not of the Catholic faith. Not all families are like this, but when this happens, it leaves people with the feeling that they are letting down their family. They feel shame and guilt like they are doing something wrong. This has made their recovery journey harder and questioned or destroyed their spiritual well-being. Not all go back to addiction because that support system broke, but some are not strong enough and eventually go back to it. Some have even told me they were put in a spot where they had to choose between their family or continue going to a different church or a support group within the church.

Maybe this has happened to you, maybe not, but I believe there are some learning curves of this thought in your recovery, which is why I am writing it. We need to be very careful with who we share our dreams and journey with. Not everyone will support you, and I am not saying this to discourage you. I'm only trying to make you realize that your recovery journey can get really rough, especially if you don't have that support system in your corner.

And even tougher when it's your family that turned their backs on you. I hope this is something you don't experience, but I had learned very quickly that people were not for me when I was an addict; they talked about me. Guess what? They are still not for me because I follow Christ and do his will, coming from outside and inside the church. You need to understand and know that not everyone will be for you, and that's okay. I want you to be strong, grow in your faith, and know why you do what you do in your recovery and who you do it for.

And when we feel that disconnect or our support system fails, it goes back to why you are really making this journey of recovery. To please others? For your own life? I will say this. Since I've been a Pastor and I have had many of these conversations. Your life with Christ (your salvation is what we call it) is not in a building or a certain denomination. It's in Jesus Christ alone! And I am sorry if you have ever been told you were wrong in changing your life because it wasn't in a way people thought you should change it or what they believe you need to follow.

What I experienced in that Doctor's office could have discouraged me. It could have made me think, *Was this eye doctor right? Did I really experience Christ in that church?* It could even make me question if my recovery is real.

Let me ask you this. If everyone disowned you and you were clean and sober, could this be enough for you? Could you stand alone?

Could your newfound life keep you going? If you're a Christian, could having Jesus in your clean and sober life be enough for you? I hope so! Those who you thought would support you will stop, and those you thought wouldn't support you will stand by you. People will try to discredit what is happening in your life, especially if you're going to church to better yourself. I say it all the time, "Jesus is my rehab," and I don't apologize for that. Neither should you.

My prayer is that none of this happens. I pray your support group is solid and your family keeps supporting you. Keep on in this journey, friend! You have come too far to go back. Keep pressing through! I am 100% behind you

Much love,
Anthony Torres

"God does His best work in our

hearts when we are alone because

we don't hear everyone else's voice

but His"

LETTER 23

THOUGHTS ABOUT
'YOU NEED TO BE OKAY BEING ALONE'

One muggy, hot day in Oklahoma, I jumped on my bicycle to get myself some Ramen noodles and gummy bears at the store. After parking my bike with sweat running down my face and my shirt getting damp from the weather, I had an elderly lady look at me like she felt sorry for me. Was it just me, or did she really feel this way? She had that look on her face like, *I wonder what his story is.* Why? Was it because I was riding a bike? Did I have "I AM ALONE AND MISERABLE" written on my forehead?

The truth is I have never felt more alone in my life like I did in that time in recovery. I moved to Oklahoma to be closer to my family and get away from my toxic environment, but every family member had their own lives, work, kids, and daily duties. How many of you know that you could still be around people and still feel alone? I was getting used to going to the movies alone, eating alone, shopping alone.

But I knew I was not truly alone. I knew God was with me in my newfound life. But physically, this was how I felt. I guess the whole purpose of writing this thought is that you need to be okay being alone in your recovery.

You should be able to go through your emotions alone with nobody to hold you. You should have the strength to cry alone with no shoulder to cry on. You should be okay with waking up alone and doing life alone.

But trust me when I say that even though this is an awful feeling, I believe it is where you need to be. Being alone is the lowest place to be, but this will be the best time you search, reflect, and find (I will talk more about this later). The best time for you to put in work to get where you need to be in this life of recovery is now. Nothing is competing with your time.

Let's analyze our life for a minute. Our whole life, we have been around people, whether our family or friends. We live a life controlled by a schedule or a life busy with addiction. Let's be honest; a life of addiction can be pretty busy.

But now, we find ourselves in this place of being alone. For me, I never knew I was putting myself in situations I shouldn't have been by removing myself from my toxic environments and moving away from people that were not a good influence in my life.

But what I learned is that there are toxic environments everywhere. There are toxic people everywhere you go. Going to a different state or city doesn't change that.

Here is some hard truth I need you to hear. The problem is not the environment we are in; it's you. How you deal with your emotions right now in your recovery will make all the difference in your life.

One time, I relapsed because I felt alone, and I woke up the next morning, feeling emptier than I did the night before. I didn't even like getting high. I was just bored, alone, and I needed something to do. That is a poor excuse, I know, but that was what happened to me. You know what happens when we are alone, right? We think more! Our minds take us to places we don't want to go to or places we came out of. Sometimes we go to the "what if" stage. "If I had done this____." (Fill in the blank) Once that happens, our minds start wandering and taking off. The moment that starts, it's hard to get our minds back.

Then, I would go back to church, angry and bitter at God, and ask him questions like, "Hello, I have a newfound life in you; why are you not helping me with my addiction?" Now, I look back at how foolish that was. I was asking for help, and he was doing his part, but I was not doing mine or keeping my end of the bargain.

Being alone does one thing; it makes you search deep in your heart for why you want to be alive. I know that sounds odd to you, and you may not want to hear that right now. But sometimes, God does His best work in our hearts when we are alone because we don't hear everyone else's voice but His. He is not competing with our time; we are His.

Have you ever tried to explain something to someone sitting next to you during a professional football game? Imagine the noise in the crowd. You have to lean in closer to explain so they can hear you better and more clearly. You even find yourself repeating your own words till the person understands because the noise is too loud.

This is why you are alone. Sometimes God has to get us away from the noise, from the crowd, from the busyness of addiction so he can now speak to us. It's almost like he says, "Do I have your attention now?" And the question is, what are we learning? For me, God was teaching me that I was a selfish person, an angry man, a man that held on to so much for so long. A man that had so much pride and ego. A man that had been doing things his way for too long. The only way He could get my full attention was for me to fall flat on my face, strip everything I loved and had.

He was teaching me that I was like a jar made out of clay, and He was showing me that I had a lot of leaks! My jar was cracking all over, but do you know the great thing about a jar made out of clay? It can be fixed. It can be reshaped. It may look broken, but it can be fixed.

I want to address the feeling of being alone because this could happen or might be happening to you right now. What you do with this moment will make all the difference in life. I heard many people say that being in jail or prison changed them. Why? It is because they were in that place of being alone. Maybe you are not in prison, but you feel alone. I made up my mind that it was just Christ and me, and that was all I needed? Do we like being alone? No! Do we like talking to ourselves? No! Do we like waking up every single day by ourselves? No! Do we love having every breakfast, lunch, and dinner alone? Of course, not

But this is where we are now, and you will eventually see it was a place you needed to be.

Will you relapse? I hope you won't, but I did. When I talked to people who relapsed, most of them said they got bored and felt so alone, so they went back to drugs because their mind wandered; that pain came back, and they had to use. You need to embrace this time, friend. Don't miss any opportunity to get better and keep this journey of being sober and clean alive. I wish I could have done things differently to get more in touch with my inner self. In retrospect, I see that if I had changed some things, I wouldn't relapse when alone. Let's stay in it, friend. Being alone won't last forever; you have to believe. It's just a stepping stone to take us to where we are going. So embrace the alone time; it's meant to get you better and strong!

Much love,
Anthony Torres

"That "one more" is serious business;

it can change our lives and alter

the lives of people around us"

LETTER 24

THOUGHTS ABOUT
'JUST ONE MORE'

One morning after waking up in a hotel (I stayed in many of them throughout my addiction), I looked down on my shirt and noticed a little bit of blood on the bottom of my shirt. As I turned my head, it felt like someone was stepping on it. I got up slowly and began to cough and gag. I had so much phlegm from those cigarettes or Black and Milds. I coughed, and my chest hurt. I needed to throw up, but I needed to see why I had this blood on my shirt. I put my hands in my pocket and brought out a napkin. As I wiped my nose, I noticed blood on the napkin. I then realized my nose had been so raw and dry from all the cocaine from the night before. It was another hard night for me. It was one of those mornings I used to wake up and say, "Why did I even wake up? If only these eyes would shut and never open again."

I didn't remember what I did the night before, but It was 6 am, and I needed more cocaine. It didn't matter how sick I felt; I always needed more. I couldn't go back home, I was a mess, and I didn't want my kids to see me this way. I would sleep when my body shut down after being up for a few days. I figured staying in a hotel was better for my family. They didn't need to see me this way.

Letters To My People

One of the times I was apart from my kids, I had not seen them for some days, and my parents had them for the week; they saw me at Buffalo Wild Wings' bar while they were having dinner with my parents. I was out partying the night away. I had probably been up for a few days like a walking zombie drugged out. This was when Sasha left me, so I probably hadn't eaten or slept in days; that time was really hard for me. My mom did say I looked horrible, like I hadn't eaten in days; I didn't look like her son. And Iliana noticed me right away. She said, "There is my daddy. I'm going to say hello." My mom said, " No, Illiana, not right now." My mom said she was despondent and confused when she said that. Can you imagine what was going through Iliana's little heart? Why? *Why can I not say hello to my daddy?*

I wonder what was on Iliana's little mind when she went back to her grandma's that night. Can you imagine being a child with such a deep love for your parents, then you are told you couldn't say hello to one of them when you saw them, or you couldn't be with them for the weekend, or maybe supervised visits? I can't even imagine what I put my kids through because I chose to chase my drugs and alcohol over chasing them.

If there is one thing that you and I are so good at in our addiction, it is "just one more." Just one more beer. Just one more high. Just one more party. Just one more night. But I wonder how many people have died of an overdose because of just one more.

I wonder how many days we could get back or how many difficult nights or days we could have saved ourselves and our families if we just didn't have one more. It's the one more that gets us in trouble. It's the one more that gets us in jail. It's the one more that hurts or kills us.

The purpose of this thought is to let you think of your urge for "one more." I really want you to dig deep and see what you need to change. I don't want you to have one more, but get on this road of recovery. I am not trying to scare you with this thought, but I need you to think because the choice is yours. Do you know how many people I have had this same conversation with in my office? Whenever they choose to have one more, I always ask, "What if that one more kills you when you could have stopped?" They reply with, "I know I need to stop. It is just hard."

Then I say, "That is why it's called addiction. Do you need a long-term or short-term facility?"

I then get the, "I will get back to you on what I want to do" response.

Months later, I hear they are back in jail, in prison, or overdosed and died.

That "one more" is serious business; it can change our lives and alter the lives of people around us. I look back on my life, and I'm always grateful for how one more didn't kill me. Even though it got rough for me in the end, there were some things that I really had to look at and see how I could get better and change my life.

When I was in rehab, some men in one of the corner rooms were trying to get drugs in the rehab home. Think about how silly and desperate that sounds. Even though they were in rehab trying to kick drugs, they still needed just need one more. The power and stronghold that drugs have on us are just breathtaking and alarming. Throughout this book, I will share how you can have NO MORE!

Much love,
Anthony Torres

"If I relapsed, I kept going. If I went backward, I kept going. If I failed so badly, I kept going"

LETTER 25

Thoughts about
'Relapse'
"Will I Always Be This Way?"

Relapse! I wish it were not a part of recovery, but sometimes, it is. Some quit cold turkey, some struggle in recovery. It's that everyday battle for many. I know I relapsed, and times like that almost made me not want a sober and clean life anymore. But I knew that was wrong thinking. People make a lot of discoveries on their recovery journey. Some find God, and some don't. Mine was finding Christ, but it's something that I struggled with at the beginning because it came down to questions I would ask Him. I asked questions like, "If you're so powerful and mighty, why can't I stop doing drugs like now?" "Why can't I stop going out and making a mess of myself?" I had many of those conversations weekly.

Of course, He would be silent, and I would ask those questions again when I prayed. It was three weeks since I started going to church, and I was still unsure about this new church-life. I was learning to adjust to it.

Relapse was a part of my recovery, and I am sure it is or was a part of yours. If it's not, that is super awesome for you! Hopefully, you will keep reading to see how you can help others.

One night after church, I remember getting so high and drunk that I couldn't even remember what happened that night. All I remember was waking up on the floor with my Bible in my hand. Was I reading God's word drunk? Was I trying to find answers in a spot where I felt low and alone? I remember feeling so sick to my stomach that all I did that day was throw up and ask God why. But my whole thought process had changed from "I just really want to die, I hate my life," to "I really need help up there, sir. God, will I always be this way?" Sometimes it was just a scream of "HELP, " or "When will this addiction, this desire in my body go away?"

I bet if you have relapsed, you were probably asking yourself those questions also. I want you to get all those negative thoughts out of your mind when you relapse. It doesn't mean defeat for us unless we want it to. But your life is not over yet. These setbacks in life are meant to help us, not break us. But it is just how we view it. There were mornings I would wake up with a bottle full of emotions that I couldn't even stand the sight of myself in the mirror. *How will I overcome this? Will I relapse again? Why can't I just stop ruining my life already?*

But here is the thing, I kept going—hour after hour, day after day. If I relapsed, I kept going. If I went backward, I kept going. If I failed so badly, I kept going. In my worst thoughts and my lowest days, I kept going. The worst thing you can do is mess up and just stay stuck. The worst thing you can do is give up and go back. Allow your setbacks to shape your future, not add more to your present. You will never see growth or results that way.

When all my four kids first learned to walk, I remember standing them up and seeing them take a few steps; it was challenging for them. But what always encouraged me was that they somehow found themselves falling with every three steps they took. Although they fell, there was the confidence to take three steps. They got back up again because they wanted more than three steps; they wanted five. But they kept getting back up and moving forward no matter how hard they fell. No matter how many times they fell, they were determined; they were confident!

I don't care how many times you have been to jail, prison, rehab, or how many times you relapsed, failed, or fell. Keep going and get back up! Be determined and confident that you can have a sober and clean life. Don't be happy with one or two steps; get to three. No matter how hard it gets, keep going!

I get it! All those negative emotions in your head and people so close to you telling you that you will always be this way. I mean, so much is against you right now. But you are in a great place because you have no choice but to get back up again and get moving

Do you know why I was relapsing? Because I was not doing my part. I was still around the same crowd, same friends, same environment, and same toxic people.

Church was the only thing that changed in my life. I just belonged to something, but I never gave it a chance to help me. It just became a part of my problem. But once I started to put things in order and discipline myself (which I will talk about later in the book), guess what I started to see? Results! And so will you if you do the things you are supposed to do, friend.

I want you to get this in your heart right now. Having a life of consistent recovery will take a life of consistent discipline. PERIOD! Your old way wasn't working, and you need to have a new way of thinking, a new way of life, a new way of doing things, so you don't keep going back to what you know. But nobody will make you do it. You have to put things in motion in your life for this to happen. Do you ever wonder why MJ was so great? He worked hard and disciplined himself. Tom Brady of *the Patriots* did the same thing. You don't get results

151

by being idle, lazy, and inconsistent. You get results by putting in work, friend. You get results by working hard and moving forward.

I can't count how many times I relapsed, and sometimes, it was right before church. Can you imagine that?

Getting high before sitting down and worshiping God. Doing a line of coke and looking at porn right before sitting down and reading the Bible.

I don't know if God heard my relapsed heart or wanted me in my sinful ways. But I know he saw my tears of struggle. I don't know if my voice reached heaven, but I know my cry reached His heart! I don't know if He gave up on me, but I was not going to let go of Him. Relapse was a part of my journey, and I am sure it is or was a part of yours.

But you can't get to a place where you don't see things working fast enough. You can't get to a place where you see the struggle but don't see the breakthrough! You can't get to a place where you think you will never have a sober and clean life. You need to keep going, keep believing, and keep at it!

A solid tree doesn't fall with one chop of the ax. Eventually, it will fall with every chop of the ax. We never know how many chops it will take; all we know is that we are closer to the tree falling with every chop. We just keep swinging till the tree falls. Keep chopping, brother and sister!

Keep swinging even if the ax gets heavy at times. See your addiction fall with every chop.

I know you can do it! I wanted to get this book in your hand so you can hear some stranger tell you that he believes in you. I'm cheering you on from here in Alamogordo, NM. There is no magic wand you can wave around to make everything go away. We have to put in some serious work, but the whole point of writing this is to encourage you in your journey.

It is okay if you relapse. It is okay if you fall backward. Just get up and get going again, don't stay stuck. Get moving! And no, you won't always be this way!

Much love,
Anthony Torres

"You can't share your family with your addiction; it will overshadow your family"

LETTER 26

THOUGHTS ABOUT
'ADDICTION VERSUS FAMILY'

If there is one thing addiction does, it tears a family apart, little by little, day by day, pain by pain. You wake up one day and realize you spent years trying to get things right in your family. I say it all the time; Sasha leaving me was the best thing that could have happened. It was hard for her. I mean, who wants to separate the family like that? But she was tired, she deserved the best in life, and I wasn't giving her that.

The purpose of this thought is to let you know you can't have your addiction and your family at the same time. It's too much stress on you, your family, and those who love you. In some sense, your drug is your mistress. It's a side thing you do when in need, and eventually, it will catch up with you.

You can't share your family with your addiction; it will overshadow your family. When Sasha left me, I had some choices to make. It was either I get better, or I continue and eventually kill myself!

This thought also aims at giving you hope that God can restore your family. If you're still with your family, that is great! I want you to get better. I don't want them to leave you in your addiction, but get help now.

What you don't know is that Sasha and I split up for four months. It was our first time apart. She had put up with my addiction for almost nine years. If there is one thing we both understood during our separation, it is that family is so important.

While Sasha was trying to figure out her own life, starting all over, I tried to figure out mine and tried to get better. During my first week in rehab, I would open my eyes and reach out to see if she was there on the other side of the bed, but it was empty. And when I reached, all I could feel was cold sheets in an empty room. She wasn't there, she was gone, and it took me a while to adjust to that. I missed her smell. I missed her touch. I missed everything about her. If your family left you, I want to give you some thoughts in *Release and Heal* later on in the book.

I had to let her go and started healing in my heart. That was hard for me because my family was everything to me, and I messed that up. But I needed to move on with my life. I was dreaming about something that was never going to happen, which was getting my family back.

In church, I would put her name on the prayer card, which would read, "God, please bring me back my family. I am sorry I hurt your angel."

I think the State taking custody of a woman's kids because of her addiction is the hardest thing a mother can go through. A father not allowed to see his kids due to addiction as well can be saddening.

When I was in rehab, I heard the screams of a mother in the other room saying, "NO, please don't take my babies away. I am getting better." Or a father sobbing on the other end of a phone, saying, "Please let me see my kids. I haven't seen them in months, I am sorry."

I know this hurts because it has gotten to this point in your life. We had options; drugs or our family. And sadly, we see the power that drugs have had in our lives. The reality is that those addictions ended up deciding for us. How many times did we say this will be the last time? How many times did we break promises?

I know our first reaction when things go bad in our lives is getting upset and being angry at who left us or turned their back on us or maybe being bitter in the situation that we are in. But remember, something had to be given.

As I sit down and write this, I think about how many birthdays I missed out on because I spent my time and energy trying to find the next high, trying to get the next 20 pack, trying to make sure that I didn't lose out on all the fun and parties.

Physically, I might have been there, but mentally, I was checked out. I think about how many times I missed out on being in the moment with my kids when they blew out the candles on their birthday cakes or how many award ceremonies I missed out on in school because I was never mentally around.

Holidays are meant for Thanksgiving and spending time with families. Sadly, I was high and drunk at every Thanksgiving. Instead of helping out to cut turkey, I was cutting lines. Instead of holding my family so tight, I was holding my beer can. Instead of being in the moment with my family, I was looking for the next party. I wish I could say I did this for months, but it was for years. If we are not careful, we can blink and see years go by. The whole purpose of writing my thoughts in this book is to try opening the eyes of the addict before things get too far and too late in your life.

I know you don't like where you are today; it will be one of the most challenging places you can ever be when it comes to losing your family or kids.

Something was missing in your life, and you are in this spot you are in. But if you are reading this, you now have a choice again. It is not over for you. It is just the beginning of doing things right. Every day, we are always left with choices to be made, but I don't believe you want to stay where you are. Neither do I believe that you don't ever want to see your kids again. Now, you have the opportunity to make a life-changing choice. You either be the one who overcomes this addiction or the one who will always be defeated in life.

Today, you can choose to live a clean and sober life with your family or keep allowing drugs to plague your life.

While in rehab, one thing that struck me so hard was that I really lost everything I loved and had. No house, no vehicle, no job, no direction, NOTHING. Not even my family! Material things can always be replaced, but that doesn't apply to family. Did I want my kids to be raised by another man? NO! Did I want Sasha to be with another man? Absolutely not! But I knew from there on out, I had some life-shaping decisions to make.

Even if I never got my family back, I still would have to choose between my family and addiction in the future. This is because the decisions you make now will set you up for the future. Even if Sasha never came back, I knew I needed to change and be better for my future partner. I believe in my spirit and heart that you will make the right choices. I believe in my heart that once you start to make those healthy choices for your life, you will begin to see things come together. Even if you don't see it happening right away, continue to make wise choices, good choices.

Today, make a stand to choose family over addiction

Much love,
Anthony Torres

"This part is so important in your

recovery process, and no matter

when your past comes up, keep

pressing through"

LETTER 27

THOUGHTS ABOUT
'IT WILL CATCH UP'

It was 2019, and I got some news that took me some time to digest and process. It was news that made me depressed for four days. I think if we are sincere, we all have been there before. My prayers felt like they were falling on deaf ears, my readings felt empty, and with embarrassment, I shut down

I was warring in my own mind. The Doctor said, "Your liver is 30%-40% scarred." Of course, the doctors don't give you the best news on what can happen next. As a matter of fact, they tell you every worse case possible. I was 224 pounds, and I was overweight. Of course, my next thought was *WHY?* I had been clean and sober for ten years. If any, I should have a healthy liver. How many years would I have to live before my liver gives out? Five years? Ten years?

During those four days, God and I begin to talk. During those conversations, I would cry, get angry and ask why. I would say things like, "I gave up everything for you. Is this how you repay me?" or "I have sacrificed so much for you. I did everything you asked of me. WHY this?" Of course, he was silent. And I would find myself having Job's moments from the Bible. I think if we are all honest, we all have been there before. Some of us just don't want to admit it.

But on my last day of feeling sorry for myself, He began to speak to me. It was as clear as day. He said, "You did this, not me. I gave you free will; what you did with it is on you."

Then it hit me like a ton of bricks. My past caught up with me. Every pill I popped, every cocaine and heroin line I snorted, every drink I had, every shot at the bar, every ice I smoked, every prescription pill smashed and snorted had caught up with me. Every night I heard, "Last call for alcohol," all the nights at the strip club, all the nights at the club with lights flashing in my face and dancing the night away to my favorite song had caught up with me. All the late-night motor-cycle rides, hopping from one bar to another, had caught up with me. All the late-night taco munchies at Jack in the Box, all the throwing up, all the sleepless nights had finally caught up with me. All the hungover mornings, all those years of damaging my body had hit me all at once.

Once again, my past was peaking its ugly head in my present; it was messing with my future and reality. God was not to blame; nobody was to blame. There is truth in the saying, "What you sow is what you reap."

So I peeled myself off the couch and did what I tell the church to do; seek the heart of God, pray, and read His word. I licked my wounds and moved forward. I got my thoughts together, got my spirit checked. I got my heart right with God, and the next day, I made the needed decision to take my health back. Within the next four months, I lost over 28 pounds. Now I am still in it today and unsure about what the future holds, but I know who holds the future.

The past is an ugly beast, isn't it? Jail time, probation, health issues, broken relationships; the list is endless when it comes to our past. When we flirted with darkness, we just jumped right in with two feet. When we played with fire, we were okay if we got burned. Sometimes the past will chase us, but I hope you can run the race. If your past catches up with you, you're no longer you. This is an area you need to be strong in, right now, at this moment, because we never know when our past will try to come up. I can't tell you how many times people have thrown my past in my face. It's like they are stuck there, they haven't moved on, and they always want to remind me of who I was or how I hurt them. My past has tried to come back several times.

If I wasn't strong enough, I could have said, "Forget this," and gone right back to my old ways. Of course, this is a choice we all have. But hopefully, when your past tries to come up again, you won't let the sting begin, you won't let the thoughts pierce you, you won't let the whispers get louder than your purpose, you won't let that cloud begin to cover you.

If there is anywhere I want to help you get to; then it is a place where you can find purpose. Ten years ago, who would have thought God would hand-picked this tattooed Latino to pastor a growing, thriving church? The fact that God even allowed my voice to have influence still blows my mind and takes my breath away. From waking up with no purpose to waking up with a purpose in my heart, helping whoever I can.

Do you know how many times I cursed God with this voice? Do you know what He brought me out of? Do you know how many shameful and embarrassing acts I had committed? Yet He hand-picked me! I am nothing, but I just continued to let Him use me however He sees fit.

And He wants to do the same with you. God does not see our past; He sees our future. You may not feel like you have a purpose or value in your life because of all the drunk and high nights or years in prison. You may not feel you have a purpose because of the things you did, but if you pay attention to anything in this book, the message is that YOU HAVE PURPOSE! I want you to find it. I want you to dig so deep in your life and start pursuing it. This part is so important in your recovery process, and no matter when your past comes up, keep pressing through.

Most of the time, I counsel people who have to deal with old charges; deal with it! Don't run from it. I learned that the more we try to run from our past and not deal with it, the more it keeps coming for us. But wouldn't it be great if we don't have to look over our shoulders anymore? I know it's easy to just ignore it and not deal with it, but face it with courage and strength. Face it with Christ in your heart!

Right now, you might be discouraged because of your past, but don't be. You might have gotten some news just like I did and want to stay down. The judge maybe didn't show you mercy, and now you're in jail for a while, don't get discouraged. I don't know what my future holds; I honestly don't know how many more years I have left with my family. I don't know if I will start to have issues later. I just don't know! But I believe I still have a purpose. I believe God can heal me if He chooses to, but I'll keep moving forward till then. I keep working for Him. I keep trying to be the best father and husband I can be every day. I make the best of the second chance He has given me.

I can't wait till you find your purpose. I want to hear all about it! Remember, you don't have a past; you have a future!

Much love,
Anthony Torres

My Journey to Recovery.

"Recovery is hard. Regret is harder." – Brittany Burgunder

"Your 'now what' plan must not break you more than it makes you; it should rather challenge and stretch you"

LETTER 28

THOUGHTS ABOUT
'NOW, WHAT?'

F irst, let me say *thank you* for taking out time to read this book. It's been ten years in the making, and I must say that I feel so nervous about sharing my heart and life with the world. I hope I haven't bored you too much? I am sure some things were hard to read, but I also hope they have helped you, or at the least, made you think about some areas of your life that need to heal. I don't think my story is that important, but I'm certain that God put it in my heart to get this book out. Undoubtedly, the journey has been filled with ups and downs. Trust me; I have traveled many roads with these tired and blistering feet. So the question that always pops up when people want to get sober and clean is: Now what? Where do I begin?

You might be in jail, a rehab, a place to get better, or you just might be sleeping on your friend's sofa; whatever the case is, you can hear echoes of that same thing. "What do I do when I get out?" "What do I do now?" Remember, I was already going to my third month without seeing my kids. No job, no money, no vehicle, nothing! You will hear that word a lot because that's what addiction does to you. It leaves us with absolutely nothing. I rode a bicycle sometimes to get me where I needed to go, but I often walked or got rides and asked myself this same question. Now that I have decided to commence this journey to being clean and sober, what now?

Well, first, it starts with a plan! Ask yourself this, where are you going, and how will you get there? When you plan a long road trip, you don't just jump into a car and go. You have a plan; you put gas, air the tires up, check the oils, make sure the vehicle is ready for the trip. Then you see which route you will take to get to your destination. This is no different; you need a plan before you embark on the journey to recovery. I know it feels like you got 10 million things going on, and you are not sure where to start. This reminds me of a hurricane that leaves behind the remains of debris everywhere, and the city is left to pick up the pieces. In the same vein, you will have people picking up the pieces of their lives, house by house, piece by piece—life by life.

Your addiction — your past — has left that for you anyway. You are left with no other choice but to start rebuilding by picking it up **one piece** at a time; you may have to search and find that piece for a very long time, but it all starts somewhere. Soon, you will see your plan coming together. For me, it was my spiritual life. It was the things I needed to work on as a man, inside of me, every single day. My heart was prideful; it was full of lust and ego, hate and bitterness, unforgiveness was not exempted. For an addict, this was my sole priority in getting myself right; I had to know myself all over again. And this time, build me (inside and out) the right way, you know, work on my inner self more. So, I began to work out, run and build my physical body; I had damaged it for too long. Then, the next was trying to find a job to provide for myself and my kids. Everyone's plan will be different, but these were some of the things I started with. Don't they say a journey of a thousand miles begins with a step?

Your plan might be trying to get off probation, finish your jail sentence, or get out of rehab. Whatever the case may be, don't wait to get out to start this plan. You need to start now, get a pen and paper, and begin noting things down. A plan keeps you focused, keeps you motivated, keeps your priorities straight! I believe it will put you on the path to being clean and sober. But one key thing I learned in the 'now what?' phase is that we want the 'now' to hurry up a little faster so we can see the big picture of our lives. See, it's the 'now what?' phase that will test our patience in our life of recovery.

If you did not hear anything today, hear this: "TRUST THE PROCESS." When you rush the process, you can get yourself in trouble.

Think about this for a second. You were in addiction for what? Ten years? Twenty? Maybe a few years. It will take you a little longer to see your 'now what' plan come into full motion. But, not to worry, it starts with your dedication to getting the best version of yourself. In your 'now what?' phase, you will have to do a lot of deep soul-searching and a thorough search into your heart. You will hear me say this throughout the rest of the book. Not only do some things in your life need to change; **all things need to change**. The way you go about planning and working on this is totally up to you.

Your 'now what' plan must not break you more than it makes you; it should rather challenge and stretch you. I repeat, it must not break you to the point that you work so hard to go back and give up. Things won't be handed over to you. You have to work toward it, every second and every minute of your life. There will be some things in life you will have to adjust if the plan gets altered. For example, I never thought of moving back to New Mexico since I started working on my life. As far as I was concerned, I was focused on staying in Oklahoma and digging my roots there, settling, finding a career, and maybe even starting a family. After all, it was my home, my place of birth, and my family was there.

Of course, I needed my kids, and my kids needed me as well. But moving back home to New Mexico was not in my plan. So I had to adjust; relapsing was not in my plan, but I had to adjust. Living without money was not my plan, but I still had to adjust. Going back home to find Sasha dating someone else was never in my plan, but I had to adapt and let her go. I had to learn how to handle life in a completely new way by being sober and clean, and so would you, my friend.

Again, living with my parents once again was not in my plan. I had to adjust and be thankful I had a place to stay. I think you get what I am saying. In your plan, you're going to have to adjust. In our recovery, we don't like to adjust; we prefer to play safe; as long as we stay in our 'bubble,' we are good, and we feel secure. But if you're going to get on this road to being sober and clean, listen to me; you're going to have to do a lot of ADJUSTING. Sometimes, that bubble pops, and we have no choice but to adjust some things in our lives. I believe you can and will do it.

So after your 'now what?' phase, the next thing is to SET YOUR GOALS. Again, this will look different for everyone. My goals right away were to go back to school and get my Master's Degree in Christians Counseling to help those struggling with addiction. I set goals to get a steady job, get healthy, and become a better father to my children.

A plan keeps you focused, but goals keep you going! It's not just waking up and having the mentality of "whatever today brings." No! You have to control your day with your goals. My kids will tell you my favorite saying is, "Today, you will put in work". Whatever that looks like for you, I want you to do it with passion and purpose.

These are some things I started to do early on my recovery journey that helped me: a plan followed up with goals is crucial, friend—getting things in the proper order for your life. Today, you have to set yourself up to WIN! Put yourself in a position to win, don't put yourself in place to lose. We know what that looks like, but WINNING is a different ball game; it requires a different strategy. It is something we are not used to, but you're already a winner in my book for wanting to get sober and clean; taking that first step that is always the hardest.

It is in the 'now what?' phase that you will find out how far you can push yourself physically and mentally. For me, it was a phase where I had to find out who I was, a place that I had never been before. I was used to drinking and waking up with a hangover, snorting coke till my nostrils bled, popping pills till I went higher, smoking ice till my eyeballs popped out of my sockets. Those were the things that constituted my day most of the time, and I was okay with that. I felt like I was just coasting in life. Have you ever felt like that?

But I didn't want to coast anymore. I wasted years of my life coasting that I couldn't get back, and now I was set in whatever the future had for my kids and me. I was God-focused; I was driven like never before. Something in my heart was ignited, and I needed to keep feeding it! I didn't want to die in my addiction. I was in a position to win, and it felt good for once, and my only enemy would be myself.

That is the scary part about life; our reflection. We have the power to quit or keep going, be idle, or keep pushing through. This is what I want for you; you should be so driven and motivated that nothing will get in your way. Not even your addiction!

In your 'now what?' phase, you can look back and see how it made you stronger and better. It is the times you didn't know how things were going to be but kept trusting God and moving forward no matter what. The time is NOW!

Lace-up your bootstraps, pick up your big girl/big boy pants, and get ready to learn how you can scale through the course to being sober and clean. Let's go!

Much love,
Anthony Torres

"To experience the NEW life, you have to let OLD things heal"

LETTER 29

Thoughts about
'Old Wounds can Heal'

I t was a cold fall night in 2009 in Las Cruces, and Thanks-giving was to be held here. It would be my first time alone on holiday. But it was my typical Thanksgiving where I watch my Cowboys play, after which we all have an afternoon of drinking. I could only spend a few hours with my kids as Sasha and I were still split up. After being in Oklahoma for some time, I was home because I felt that I needed to come home to my kids, who I had missed so much. I had found my new-found faith in Christ, but I seemed to be still struggling with my addictions and past. The good news was that I looked at life differently, and my drug use was not as aggressive as it was in that year, I would still drink, but I didn't even enjoy it as much anymore.

It was one of the worst Thanksgivings I have ever had; be-cause once the kids left, I was alone, and I had to think about a whole lot of things. I am not sure if you have ever gotten to a place in your life that even though everything was falling apart around you, even though things in your life were not how you thought they would be, you were at some sense of peace within your own heart.

That was me at that moment. Even though I didn't like where I was at that moment, and I felt I was starting my life all over again, even though I felt like I was alone, I was at peace for once in my life. Peace was something that I lacked in my 28 years of being alive, but I was at complete peace, the perfect peace, and I thank God for that. I was going to make it, and everything was going to be okay.

I believe Sasha was at peace as well, and word on the street was that she was getting engaged, which was a shocker to me, considering we were only apart for four months. I believe that when you move on and allow the wounds of life to heal, you leave things behind. You have known your whole life that things don't work out as planned. I guess you know what you want in life, then go for it. The truth is, I was happy for her and her newfound life, even if it wasn't with me.

When she would pick up the kids from me on my days, I would make sure I made her a cup of coffee with a note stuck to it that said: "I love you and God bless." Of course, I wouldn't get the reaction that I wanted, but that only lasted a few weeks before I stopped. The truth is I think I needed to move on with my life, and I needed to let go; I just didn't know how to. I just wanted her to know the God that I knew truly. Then one day, I just stopped fighting for her. I knew if we got back together, it would be an act of God, not an act of my emotions. I prayed for her daily and prayed blessings for her life. There was so much hurt for both of us; we would relive too much pain if we made things work out. A lot of healing would need to take place.

Anyway, I would date when I needed to, make new friends when I was out, but I was only trying to get better in my life. I was not a hundred percent yet, and I still had a lot of work to do because I was still barely going to church faithfully and praying things would get better in my life. At church, I would fill out the prayer cards and write: "God bring back my family. Please, I am sorry." As the days went on, the reality of that prayer was very slim. She wasn't coming back, and I needed to be okay with that.

My prayer at this time was to have a Christian woman one day that would follow this journey with me. Who would it be?

Fortunately and unfortunately, one cold crispy fall night, I got a 'My space' message, and it was from Sasha. She asked: "What happened to us?" Of course, my reply was: "I was sick, but I am getting better." Why would she send me that message? My mind began to wonder. *"Is she playing games with me? Is God answering my prayer? Why is she texting me? What is going on?"* This was just out of the blue! *"Is this a distraction to my recovery?"*

For once, my emotions were not all over the place, but with this conversation happening, I didn't know how to feel. Of course, I wanted my family back; I wanted a second chance to make things right, to prove myself. We all deserve a second chance! Was I getting mine?

After we had many talks and some complex discussions later in that week, we decided to work things out and get back together. We wanted to make things work for our family. I knew that I lost all the things up to that point; my house, truck, motorcycle, business, and money were all gone. Material things can be replaced, but my family could never be.

I wish I had a video recorder to get the expressions on the kids' faces when we broke the news to them that we were getting back together. It was priceless. That day, I truly believed that my kids began to heal in their hearts from the tornado paths of addictions. They were innocent in all of this, and they just got trapped in the wind. Unfortunately, many kids do when a parent is addicted.

One fateful day, Sasha had gone to see me at my mom's for my lunch break as we were still living in separate homes for the meantime, and I will never forget her words. She said,

"How are our lives going to look now? Can we heal from our past? How can I learn to trust you again?"

To all those honest and valuable questions, my response to her was, "All I know is I want something different for our kids and family. I want to make Jesus the center of everything that we do moving forward." The truth is, I don't even know what that means.

All I know is I have lived my life without him for so long; I don't want to live another minute without Him in my heart.

Can we heal? I believe we can! I don't know when it will begin, but I know one day, we can trust again. It is possible! There was a lot of work and healing that needed to be done on our part. There was a lot of reformation that needed to take place.

Like tornadoes leaving debris in the roadway and a family picking their house in pieces scattered in the fields due to a strong storm, we would now be a family picking the pieces of our lives from the destruction of addiction. We would pick every part, every wall, and every emotion. Our children were walking on eggshells and probably in fear that I would go back to my old ways. Probably in fear that I would walk out that door and never return. I'm sure with every night that Sasha laid her head down on her pillow, she probably looked at me and thought, "Can I trust him again?" or even a deeper question, "Is he for real?"

I know deep down inside that I was terrified. I didn't want to mess this up!

A week later, Sasha gave her heart to Christ in the church I was attending, and 22 days later, we got married. After four months of being apart, our family would be together after all the questions, the pain, and the hard times of life. Amidst all the confusion and lost moments, our family was back together again. So what is left of our lives now?

My heart and prayer are that every story ends this way because kids need their parents, and family needs to come together. I know it can be challenging because all we see is hurt, but we must also see healing.

I'm writing this because you might not think things can heal; you might not believe that things can come back together, but they will. You might not think things can be restored, but they can. If you are separated from your family, keep praying, keep believing, keep looking for better days. Once I made up my mind that I deserved to be happy and deserved a good life, I began to find peace and move forward with or without my family. Once I made up my mind that I wanted a better life and I was not looking back at my past, I began to heal. Once I took my hands off the past, I could feel things gradually getting back in place.

I knew I was always going to have my kids, but in my mind, I wasn't sure I would have everything that I lost due to addiction. I genuinely believe God changes hearts! Healing is not just for your family; it's for you as well. I knew that no matter what, I needed to heal within myself. I had spent my whole life tearing things apart. I was afraid to move forward in my new life in fear of messing things up again, but I knew that I needed to heal in many areas of my life.

I destroyed everything that my hands touched. In my senior year of high school, I was not playing my last year of football due to drinking, my career in state corrections, my dreams, my business was affected, and my family was not left out.

Yeah, I felt like a flunky, a screw-up. If I were not careful, I would be trying to figure out life in my mid-50s. In my 60s, I was still messing things up. You bet there was a lot of healing that needed to be done in my life, but it started with me taking the first step. I needed to know, and I needed to see that OLD

WOUNDS could HEAL. Do you believe it's possible for your life?

Old hurts, old thoughts, old words, old promises, old pain, old wounds, our old life can heal!

Listen to this, "To experience the NEW life, you have to let OLD things heal."

There were things in my life that I had to let go of and let God! I had to release Sasha and begin to heal for myself. But now that she was back in my life, I knew that we could heal together. Getting back together was a good thing, but all we saw was old pain when we looked at each other. We had to believe that old wounds could heal. I was thankful that my family came back to me, and my prayer is that yours will come back as well. Maybe they have, and you need to start healing together. All I know is old things, as well as old wounds, can heal. Healing is what everyone needs. We can never forget the past, but to have a successful recovery, we must heal. We must allow those wounds to begin to scar so we can move forward in our lives.

There is no magic in this, just hard work and dedication on your part. I will share things with you that I started doing for my emotional state of mind, for my healing, in my journey to staying sober and clean. Note that you can be sober and clean and still be angry, bitter, wounded with a heart of unforgiveness, and still wounded in life. We have many sober and clean people walking in their past, still walking in their old wounds—still walking around in their hurt. That will only make you a miserable person on your journey to being sober and clean, and who wants to live like that? You may not have your bottle anymore, but you still got that hurt. You may not be up for days anymore with your drug of choice, but your mind is in turmoil because you are still wounded from the past. It's like a movie playing in your head. You need to believe me when I say, "Old wounds can heal." It will take time, but it is possible for you and your family; I believe in you! Let us get our minds and heart ready for the next thought.

Much love,
Anthony Torres

LETTER 30

Thoughts about
'Sober Feelings'

Why do you hate me tonight?
I have been staring at the wall for an hour!
It's in the night you like to devour?
I have nothing to be anxious about, or do I?
But my thoughts get the best of me
Why can't my mind be free?
Is it hurt, is it betrayal, is it seasons of life?
It's nice to know everyone is asleep
While I sit here with my mind running deep
I pace back and forth, from the kitchen to the couch
I reach for the shepherd's pouch
I sit, I write, I read, NOTHING!
I am still awake. Why? Is it for something!
Sleep awaits me, but my mind derails me
I'm pleading with my sleep. Can I just get an hour, please?
I lay down and close my eyes again; geez!
My eyeballs go side to side like a pinball machine. Should
I pull back the pin again?
I open my eyes with a sigh of frustration
So I go back to negotiation; 20 minutes, 30 minutes are all I
ask
It's 4 am!
So I pray, as I see the day peaking,
For strength, for peace, for sleep!
I know there is nothing wrong with me,

I just want to be free.
Today is a new day! Tonight I will find sleep.

When I was in my addiction, I never struggled with anxiety nor sleep. But since being sober and clean, I have wrestled from time to time with it. I'm not sure if it has something to do with my calling or if it's just nights where my mind likes to stay thinking and won't shut off. I have become a very emotional person since I gave my heart to Christ years ago. I have been susceptible in the spirit; maybe this is it, I don't know. But this does not make me less Christian; it just makes me more human. There is nothing wrong with you either! Keep pressing through, and I pray we both find sleep tonight.

Much love,
Anthony Torres

"No matter how hard it gets, friend, you have to believe this and let God's voice overshadow those old voices"

LETTER 31

THOUGHTS ABOUT
'NEW IDENTITY; OLD VOICES'

Y ou have to know that your journey will look different from mine, but I can say this: we all will struggle with the same old voices.
On your road to recovery, you will have to stay focused. You have to be so focused that you are tripping over your shoes because your eyes are set on the goals that you can't see where you are walking.

Whatever your addiction was, we all formed an identity. It's what people saw; it's what people said, it's the things we felt, it's what we struggled with every time we looked in the mirror the next day. It seems it got more challenging for me to even look at myself; my reflection was what I battled the most in my mind. Maybe you are like me. I was disgusted with myself. Every time I looked in the mirror, looking at my tired face and my bloodshot eyes, I would say: "Can today be the day I get better?" Then I would spend nights messing things up with my family; I would skip the night. That was what I had become. It was like I had the devil sitting on both shoulders feeling that heaviness upon me, but listen, friend: I want you to take a deep breath and understand that this is not you anymore. I want to help you with that in this thought. You are not what people say or think! You are not what you feel but how you see yourself.

I want to talk about some voices that you're going to hear on your road to recovery, voices that you will have to shut down, voices you will have to tune out. Now and then, these voices still creep in from time to time for me, but you must overcome them. I see these as distractions. Believe it or not, distractions keep you off where you are going in life. But I want to help you with how you can healthily process those voices. So here we go:

Voice number one will be your past friends.

It should be no surprise that you're going to form some pretty solid relationships in your life of addiction. But they can't be a part of your journey if you're going to be sober and clean. They will either encourage you or discourage you; they will either support you or not; your circle of friends will be vital in this journey.

When I started to clean up, I would hear things like, "Oh, you think you're too good to talk to us now" or "We don't have anything in common, why hang out?" Was I hurt about this? Sure I was, but they say you will know your true friends when you go through a rough time in your life. Of course, some called with words of encouragement, while some never called. You have to let people say what they will say about you, and I know this would be hard for you to swallow, but you must know this now.

Sometimes you will have to let old friendships die. Stop chasing people who don't want to be a part of your recovery. Stop begging people to be a part of your new life. If they can't cry with you and hold your head up in the bad times, they don't deserve you in the winning times of your life. I have learned over the years that people's words don't mean any-thing. It doesn't impress me; your actions and support do. It's no different in your recovery; sometimes, it's best to cut those friendships for the sake of your recovery. You have too much going on already; you only need voices of friends that will support you and be there for you.

Listen, if they genuinely wanted your friendship, they would have supported you since day one; they would have been there while you were in jail, prison, or rehab. They would have been there when you fell and hit that concrete floor. I have seen it too many times; someone is doing so well in their recovery, then they get mixed up again in the old crowd, with old friends, old stomping grounds, and next thing you know, they are back to the old them again in addictions, why? Because they keep chasing friendships that they should have let go of a long time ago. Your homie is not always your homie, and your homegirl is not always your homegirl; that's street talk. Real talk is friends that support you no matter what. Let those old friendships die for the sake of your recovery. Don't give in to the old voices!

Another old voice is your family:

This one is hard! I mean, your family is supposed to be your biggest supporter. Maybe! Again, I think every situation is different. In my recovery, it was getting it right with God and going to church that helped me out. It was new to my family and me, but I was content with where I was. I had some family that supported me and some that didn't. I heard words like: "Now you're a bible thumper." "As long as you're in church, don't talk to me." "Don't preach to me!"- that one was my favorite, only because I have never been the preachy type. I didn't like it when people preach to me, so I was not going to preach to others. God had to get a hold of their lives as far as I was con-cerned as he did mine. My words were not going to mean an-ything. But I always noticed I could feel the tension when I was around my family; it got awkward sometimes. They looked at me to see if I was for real in my new life. Sadly, even to this present day, some still don't understand. But again, sometimes you have to let things be said and move forward. Family or not, you have to decide who will be a part of your life in recovery.

Does it hurt that your mom or father don't support you? Or your sister or brother that you looked up to are not there for you? Sure it does, but what I have learned earlier is that every-one within themselves deals with their varied issues- the past, their hurts, and their demons. I learned very early on not to take things so personally in life.

This one can be hard for you if you're close to your family, and you do everything together. When I started to sober up, I found myself going to fewer BBQs with family members that were drinkers; I found myself going to more occasional B-day parties or holiday dinners with my family. Again it was not that I thought I was better than anybody else; I was only guard-ing my heart and mind in sobriety. You have to and need to; if you are going to stay sober and clean, NO ONE else will do that for you. You don't want to put yourself in a spot where you are going to be tempted. It is up to you, no matter how upset your family gets you for not showing up as much; if they love you, they will understand.

Suppose some members of your family are drinkers or us-ers. Once you are out of that circle of addiction, expect that they can turn on you with hurtful words. Do not give in to those voices; you are sober and clean now. You need to guard that with every bit of energy you have, even if it means losing fam-ily. I get it! They are family, but are you willing to stay in ad-diction and die for the sake of being afraid to lose your family?

Or live life sober and clean with hopes that those relationships can be amended in time.

Now, it's been so long that I have been sober and clean. I can now be around my family even if they are drinking, only that I see them once every other year or so. I have no desire or cravings anymore. Early on, I had to watch where I was at all relevant times, and so would you, my friend.

The next one, I believe, is more complicated, but you can do once you get past these thoughts is how you can effectively handle the old voice in your mind with your new identity. When I would relapse, I would hear: "You are always going to be this way" or "You are too weak, and you will always be a loser."

Do you know how many times I thought about giving up? I will always say: "Forget this lifestyle it's too hard; I should just go back to my old self." Or how many times I would sit in the parking lot of a liquor store, in my vehicle, with my knees shak-ing, thinking about getting a bottle and getting on a binge. Or how many times I would try to remember my dealer's phone number. When I eventually pick up the phone and call him, I would hear his voice and say: "Never mind," then hang up and begin to chew my nails off to the skin. The voices were intense, and my thoughts about myself were discouraging.

That struggle is real, friend! But I had to press through those voices. I would pray, I would read, I would watch a ser-mon. I needed this change in my life, and I knew it was not going to come easy. But those old voices in your mind? You need to get past those. Because it is best and easier to go back to wherefrom you hail.

One voice that got me early on in my recovery was: "You couldn't make no one happy when you were an addict; you can't even make them happy now that you are sober and clean. Just go back to the old you."

191

On a faithful Wednesday in 2010, I had a long day at work, to the point that I thought my day was never going to end. I would work from 6 am to 6 pm, sometimes longer, but this day, I got out in time to make it to church. After church, we got home, and I really can't remember what Sasha and I started to argue about, but it got really heated. We both said things to each other that hurt each other's feelings. I remember saying: "Well, if it's going to be like this, then I should have stayed drunk and high; it seems I can't make you happy." Sasha said: "That's your choice, but I won't stick around for that."

After our argument, I was warring in my mind, body, and soul! I had this unsettled feeling in my heart. I was having second thoughts about my new life, my new identity. In all, I just think it was a long day, and I needed to go to bed to sleep it off. So I showered and went to bed.

But something happened! With the battle in my mind, coupled with the struggle in my heart, and the unsettledness of my spirit, I was lying down to sleep when Sasha came to my bedside and kissed me so gently on my cheek and said: "I Love you, I don't want to fight with you" and just like that! That war, that battle in my heart, the battlefield in my spirit all STOPPED! Sasha had always been a praying woman. I believe that night, her gentle soul helped me get over that old voice because she could have gone to bed angry like me, but she didn't! She was teaching me more about myself in recovery.

She doesn't know this, but she probably has pulled me out of more dark times in my mind than she realizes. Do we have our struggles as a married couple? SURE! We all do, but when I say she is God-sent, she is. God knew what he was doing when he heard me say: "Please bring back my family." She is an angel to me and if you're a spouse reading this book, listen! You have the key to your spouse's recovery.

But it's those voices. It's those times that you will have to press through and get past because if we are not careful, we will believe the voices of those demons over the voice of God. You will believe the voices of the past instead of the present. You can get through this. You're an overcomer; you are someone, you have purpose and value in this life. No matter how hard it gets, friend, you have to believe this and let God's voice overshadow those old voices.

Whenever I feel like those voices are getting too much for me, I like to read the bible or a good book, something I probably should have done that night. But keeping your mind sharp is going to be a pivotal contribution to your recovery.

I want to end this thought with this: You have to trust the process! You spent 10-25 years being a user. For so many years, your mind, heart, and body were abused by drugs and alcohol. Your soul was dragged through the pits of hell and torment. It's not going to take a year to rebuild; it will take some time.

It has been almost 11 years, and I am still picking up the pieces of my life. People see me and say: "Woah! He is doing great for himself." Yes, I am doing better than I was years ago as I am at peace with God, and I am no longer fighting those demons alone anymore. Emotionally, I am still healing from the wounds by allowing Christ to rebuild those areas of my heart that still hurts from time to time, making me bleed and ponder.

It is imperative to be very careful with whom you let in your life during recovery and whom you speak to about your past. I learned very early that not everyone is a friend, not everyone has good intentions, and not everyone is on my side. We get hurt by people while we are still healing inside because we allow it. People will hurt you while you're still bleeding. Sadly my circle is tiny because I know that the bigger the circle, the bigger the talk, and the bigger the hurt.

I am delivered from drugs and alcohol, but I am still healing from a lot of mental issues to which I subjected myself. This is an area I need to protect, and so do you. I hope these thoughts will help you a bit in your recovery in battling with those old voices.

Sometimes you may have to say, "Shut up, that's not me anymore." This is an area where I failed very early on in my recovery, but I learned very quickly! People will be people, and they will love to throw your past and mistakes in your face, saying hurtful things to you that make you think, sowing seeds of doubt in your mind.

You have to remember with all your soul, spirit, and heart that your past is not you anymore! Do not let people take you to a place that God has brought you out of. Keep your eyes on your present life, but also avert your thoughts to your future. Learn to get over the old voices. HEY! I am very proud of you; keep fighting the good fight. Remember, I am cheering you on all the way from Alamogordo, NM.

Much love,
Anthony Torres

"You must forgive the person in the mirror"

LETTER 32

THOUGHTS ABOUT
'REFLECTION IN THE MIRROR'

L et us face it, if we did not have to look at ourselves in the mirror, we would probably be okay with however we looked, but unfortunately, we do. Every time we fix our hair, put on makeup, brush our teeth, pop a zit on our forehead, wash our face, we see a reflection we do not like to see and reflect on who we are or what we are becoming. The mirror reflects how old we are getting, showing us our shortcomings, thereby reflecting many things in our lives. It sometimes shows us the pitfalls, challenges, and weaknesses that we need to change or overcome. It is a reflection of TIME! Time we have lost, showing us just how fast life goes for us—the reflection of good times and even bad.

I am reminded about how fast life goes every time I see more grey strands in my beard. So many times, I look at myself in the mirror, and my face screams: "LIFE!". Sometimes we wear our hurt on our face, with our pain and struggles evident in the dark circles under our eyes. Sometimes our face does SCREAM out our innermost desire for salvation. In this sea of hurt, I am still fighting. I still believe in better days and a fulfilled life of being sober and clean. That is the reflection we should see when we look in the mirror.

In this thought, if you are going to begin your road to recovery, listen to these words very carefully: *You must forgive the person in the mirror.* It sounds simple, yet many fail to do it. I stayed there for a very long time, friend, and I do not want you to either. Forgiving yourself for everything you have done will be hard, but it is rewarding once you decide and go through with it.

I know it was tough for me to look at myself in the mirror, and I wish I could say it immediately got easy, but it did not. Sometimes, your reflection will remind you of all the pain and hardship you caused others; it will remind you how much time you have spent in your addiction. It reminds you of a time that you can never get back, but you must persevere.

This is a step you cannot overlook. I know you are hurting, and you sometimes cannot stand the sight of you. The custody of your kids might have been taken away from you by the state, and you feel like a horrible mom or dad. Even your parents do not want anything to do with you. Your spouse is ignoring your calls or mail; you have court dates from old charges, and your grown kids do not want anything to do with you. If the above is your story, you are as I used to be, and I get it! You wake up every day and think, "Will the people that I hurt ever forgive me?" "Will this pain go away?" "Can I do this?"

So many questions, but you must take it a day at a time. Right now, at this moment, start making plans to forgive yourself. You cannot turn back the wheels of time to make things right; you cannot think about the "what ifs." You have to live in the NOW, consciously dedicate yourself to the healing, and live knowing that it is the pieces of your life being put back together with every breath you take.

When I started to clean up my life, I owed many people money because of my business. I was up to my eyeballs in debt due to the vehicles' repo and the locking of our home due to non-payment of outstanding debts. Sadly, we lost a lot of stuff in that home, including memories I cannot get back. I was learning to deal with depression by being sober and clean. This helped me learn to rely on Christ, and it also helped me see the hurt I caused my kids and so many other people that trusted me with their feelings.

My anxiety would get the best of me sometimes at night, and I would wake up with night sweats, or I would wake up in the morning sore and tired, feeling like my body had been fighting itself. I wanted the emotional bleeding to stop; I screamed from the core of my being. I knew the only way I could stop it was by forgiving myself.

But how do we begin? In this thought, I want to give you some ideas on how you can start forgiving yourself. This will be key to your recovery. So here we go!

The first one is your CHILDREN:

I don't know how old they are, but if you remember my letter to my kids, that was my heart and soul. And your kids need to hear yours. I know slowly they had to forgive me at their own time. I even recall sometime during recovery, one of my kids brought up my past; she mentioned how horrible of a father I was, how I was never there when they needed me. With every word that was spoken, I had to listen to how they felt, and it was like needles poking my skin. It hurt, and I felt like I bled. I could feel her anger and disappointment, and my eight years of tears stored up began to fall off my face and onto the floor. I said: "Mija, I know I did those things, and I am sorry. I cannot change the past, but I am here now. I have been through a lot to get to this point in my life. Please forgive me." I believe that was a starting point in the recuperation of our relationship, and it was a deeply therapeutic experience for both of us.

199

That is what you have to tell yourself right now. Although you cannot go back to 1990 or 2000, you are here in the present, and this is what matters. I know the older the children are, the deeper the wounds will be for them. But you have to ask for forgiveness from them and move forward because if you do not do so, you will be stuck in the continuous cycle of shame and guilt. I know it is hard, as it is going on eleven years now for me, and I still look at my kids and think about how foolish a young father I was. I still sometimes hope that they truly and genuinely have forgiven me. But I do not live in that realm of guilt and shame anymore. I am enjoying the time that I have with them, sober and clean.

If your kids have things they need to say in person or through a letter, let them vent, let them heal, and let them get out whatever it is that is stored in their hearts. But you cannot let that eat you up alive because it will if you let it. Do everything within your means to process those words in such a manner as to see their feelings and work toward understanding their grievances. Remember that it is no longer about just you anymore. Do this correctly, and later on in life, your kids will respect you for your honesty and your courage in owning up to your mistakes. It is when we do not accept responsibility for the mistakes that we make that our kids will take longer to forgive us because all they see are the excuses we give for how we hurt them. Trust me when I say our kids see right through us. The best thing to do is, to be honest with them.

One time I told my kids, "I have made my share of mistakes as a young man and a father. And in your life, you will make mistakes also". This statement is very true for everyone, so the next time you look in the mirror while you comb your hair, you can stand knowing you asked for forgiveness, and you were honest and sincere. You will realize that you somehow played a part in your kids' lives for them, which will help you begin to heal. This is an excellent place to be for both of you.

The next one will depend on whether you are with someone or not, your spouse, or any relationship you might find yourself in.

Let me start by saying this; "those wounds go so deep for our loved ones." Listen to me when I say we have no room for error in this one. Your words don't matter, but your actions will, so making amends in this area will be vital for you. If you are still with your partner, that will be even better! You have a lot of work to do with actions. Don't say you are going to do better; just do it. But making that apology is important. This is what I told Sasha when we got back together: "I am so sorry I hurt you all those years, I am so sorry I made you feel like you were nothing, I am sorry I wasted all those years that we can never get back. I am not saying that I am perfect. I still have a lot of work to do, and I know you will have a hard time trusting me again. But I hope one day to gain your trust again. I love you, and I am sorry."

This can be a start for you in rebuilding your relationship.

If you are not with your spouse and they left you, I am sorry! I know this is very painful, and I have been here before. But this is a time of some deep soul searching. Dig deep into your wanting to have a life sober and clean for yourself. For you to get better, you have to live again, friend. If you hurt someone that you love, and they don't want to speak to you. Write a letter if you're in jail or prison or rehab. If you're not and have access to a computer, email it if you know that person's email. I recall that I would start the letter off with something like, "I write this not to get back together, but to simply share my heart with you and ask for your forgiveness."

When you start the letter off like that, right away, they know you are not writing a letter wanting to get back together (even though I'm sure you want to), but this will allow them to read it and not toss it when you start like that. Be honest and sincere in the letter; owning up to our own mistakes is the key to healing for everyone. They feel like you're not hiding anything or making excuses but being honest about what you say.

Friend, once you write these letters or begin to rebuild those relationships, don't look back. The worst thing we can do is make amends, begin to heal then start talking about the past. Saying things like, "You remember that one time you did?" Don't do it! In my recovery, one thing I think Sasha and I did well was making sure not to talk about the past, neither bring up old hurts nor throw the past back in each other's faces.

Sometimes we get into those moments of disagreements and start to shoot darts at each other, and we say things like: "Yeah, will you remember that time." We knew talking about the PAST to each other would keep those wounds fresh and open, but we healed by moving FORWARD. By letting God do what He says He does- restore and heal. We let go of what we couldn't change and EMBRACED what we could.

This will help you rebuild your relationships, but it will take both of you—all of your understanding, grace, and forgiveness. So give time for those wounds to heal; it won't happen overnight. I pray for you in this area because I know how hard this is, but you both can do it. If you rebuild that relationship with your spouse, it will be ten times stronger than ever before. If you're alone, God will send you the right person for your life, and your heart will be in a better place. But stand looking in the mirror knowing you left no stones unturned. You did what you could to make amends.

Next will be your FRIENDS:
Remember I told you I had a business? I hurt many people in this respect. When I went to rehab, there were people I

couldn't pay for work. But when I cleaned up, I wrote letters to explain my situation and how sorry I was. Trust me! If I had the money to pay back, I would have, but I couldn't. All I could do was ask for their forgiveness. Some of these people were good friends of mine, and sadly I haven't spoken to them in years. I had to ask for forgiveness from my drug dealers for waking them up at 4 am or knocking on their door at 6 am for 20kg worth of drugs, or trying to find them in town while they were with their family to get my high.

Can you imagine getting those calls! I'm sure they were like: "What is up with this guy?" One time I ran into this guy at a bar, and I saw him from the corner of my eye and had to ask him to forgive me for punching him in the mouth once because I swore he sold me coke mixed with so much baking soda. I even bought him a beer to make peace! Listen to me when I say I wanted to make it right with everyone; I wanted to be at peace with everyone I hurt, but mostly be at ease in my own heart and spirit, I was a different person, and I felt this change taking place inside of me.

You might have made mistakes to friends or coworkers; do what you can to make peace with everyone. The worst thing we can do is start to clean up our lives and still be looking over our shoulders, waking up with guilt and shame. Trust me! There is no peace in that. Stand in the mirror knowing you did what you could to make peace with everyone, even if they don't accept your apology, even if they don't want anything to do with you. You can look in the mirror knowing you did your part. There is peace in that.

The last one will be your PARENTS:

My parents did everything they could to help me get better, and I thank them for it. My parents were tough as nails; they did what they could for me, and if I wasn't getting better in my recovery, that was on me. They had rules and boundaries with their home, and there was no showing up drunk or high at their home, and I respected that. Not even my guilt trip lines would work on them; when I would say, "You're going to kick your own son out on the streets? I might not have a place to stay." That didn't work with my parents; my parents would say: "You can stay here if you need to. But don't bring your drugs here." I was thankful they didn't enable me in my addiction. They stuck to their words.

Asking for forgiveness with my parents was healing for me. You know that feeling when you let someone who has always believed in you down? It was hard. But I know my parents forgave me the moment I asked for it. One time my mom said: " I can die in peace now, kid; I don't have to worry about getting that phone call that you are dead or in prison." I'm sure mom was happy I was starting to clean up my life.

Today, stand in the mirror knowing you did everything you could to make amends with everyone, every soul, every living person you honestly feel you did wrong. Some may make fun of it, see you as soft, weak or reject your words. Some may not take you seriously enough, but you can look at yourself deadly in the eyes, take a deep breath, and know you did everything you could to make peace, make amends with yourself, family, friends, and others.

And most importantly, you need to look at yourself in the mirror and forgive yourself daily! Remember this: Let go of the past, let go of what you can't change but EMBRACE what you can. The worst thing we can do is live our whole lives clean and sober and NEVER forgive ourselves. We walk around defeated, with shame and guilt. NOPE! Not today! Tell yourself today is the day you walk in a forgiven self. You deserve that much friend, we all make mistakes, but we learn from them.

This thought is very important for your recovery. Work on it daily! Ask God to give you strength; let him heal those areas in your life. Think about this; God has forgiven you already. Now, you need to forgive yourself. You can do it!

Much Love,
Anthony Torres

"Yes! You deserve good things and a good life. It does not always have to be bad in your life"

LETTER 33

Thoughts about
'You Deserve a Great Life'

G rowing up, I would say I had a good life. Of course, if I could, I would change some things. But for the most part, I was taken care of alongside my brothers and sisters. We struggled like most families do. One memory I have is when my stepdad would wake me up early in the morning on a Saturday to peel copper and smash cans to take to the yard so we can get money for food for the month. One time I remember complaining about why I had to get up so early when I could have slept in; he said: "I know you are tired, but do you want to eat? Well, this is how we would have Thanksgiving this year." After hearing that, I never complained again.

Can you imagine living in a three-bedroom, one-bath home, and there were six of us under one roof. With one bathroom, someone in the house was going to take a cold shower. Of course, I didn't have the things other kids did growing up, but I saw how hard my parents worked to provide for us. Unfortunately, I took the good with the bad. We were just a family trying to survive like everyone else.

It wasn't until I grew up and made my own path, made my own decisions in life, that I started to experience negative things, adverse outcomes, to the point that I was always waiting for bad things to happen in my life. I saw no good. Do you know what I am talking about already?

I was a teen dad at 17, not that this was a bad thing, I am thankful for my oldest daughter. I dropped out of playing football in my senior year due to alcohol, I was pretty good at it from what I was told. I ruined my career with the state due to addiction and I would have been retired by now. I drove my business to the ground due to addiction; I even lost my family due to my addiction (the times I couldn't get back.) It was like everything that my hand touched I destroyed! I never really finished anything in life. I was good at making a mess out of my life, and this sucked. I always looked down on myself because of this. I grew up with a lot of insecurity, a lot of discouragement that I brought upon myself.

It seemed like I could never do any good or see good during my drug and alcohol use. All I saw for some time in my life was bad, negative, the pain, and the ugly things of life that addiction brings. Maybe this is why I stayed in my obsession for so long. I didn't think that I deserved a good life or good things. I felt that I sowed so many bad things; good didn't even exist, not in my life anyway. Back then, I lived in Karma (which I don't believe in now). A realm of life in the belief that it was never going to get any better no matter how hard I tried to have a good one.

When I tell you I had to start all over after I got out of Rehab, I meant it. I know the struggle too well. If I didn't have a family to take me in, I probably would have been on the streets. I had nothing, no job, not many clothes, no money, no vehicle, nothing! I was lucky to get a haircut if I could. That was 2009. I had spent twenty-eight years of a rough road with no promise or hope, a route with many heartaches and shattered dreams. That dark cloud sometimes felt like it was never going to lift;

maybe I was just meant to be a man constantly drenched in the rain. I was always stepping in puddles that got in my way.

Fast forward to 2015, six years clean and sober. God now has me Pastoring! (how I got here is a long story). But what was I thinking by saying YES to this new calling in my life? I told him: "Help me with my addiction, and I will do whatever you want me to," and he did, FAST! He put me to work! I found myself in a church in Alamogordo, being the lead pastor, having no clue what I was doing. A church of only 15-20 people. What in the world could I offer this church, this city? I was a nobody; if they knew my past, would they still love me? Would they even let me lead them? Am I not like the other Pastors? Am I different? I gave it a shot anyway. I gave it everything I have. If I were going to be sold out for my addiction a long time ago, it would be for Christ and the work he called me to do.

Now here I am sitting, writing this book in 2020. God took his church from 20 people to 250-300, called Mountain View Church home, in a new building he blessed us with to grow and do more. He has opened doors for me that only He can open. He has allowed me and my family to have a platform (that comes with a lot of responsibility), a voice for Him to help others. And of course, I wake up asking myself, "do I deserve this?" Absolutely not! I don't deserve anything He does in my life. But I am honored and humbled He picked a person like me to use however He deems fit. Even though leading a church has its difficult times and challenging moments, it checks my spirit daily.

Although, leading a church is not what I thought it would be, and I am learning as the years pass, not totally aware of what it entails, my answer is still the same today: "Lord, I am a nobody, I am not worthy, but you still keep me clean and sober, I still say YES! In whatever you want me to do. My life is yours. God has blessed my family and me, and the truth is we don't deserve anything good from him. I feel like I will wake up one day, and this will all be gone, and I will be back in 2009 again. But every day, I thank the Lord for not giving up on my family and me even in times I thought of giving up on myself.

I say all this to tell you: Yes! You deserve good things and a good life. It does not always have to be bad in your life. You don't always have to wait for bad things to happen; you don't always have to live a life looking over your shoulder. Don't you sit there and think for one second that God cannot bless your life because of all the bad you have done. I don't care what your background is, how many times you have been in and out of prison or rehab; it doesn't matter how many times you have fallen, how many tattoos you have on your skin. Felon, 'junkie,' flunky, or nobody. You can still make a difference in your life in this same world and be used by God!

I think sometimes the problem is we just limit Him in our lives. We tell Him: "I can't be used with this my background." But, I promise you, He will prove you wrong.

I told my wife something a while back that I just can't get out of my head. I told her, "I am afraid because everything is going so well for us; we have worked so hard to get here in our lives with our family. Who would have thought we would be here in our lives being used by God to make a difference some-how?" What if I mess everything up?

She said: "The difference between back then and now is you didn't have God in your life."

It was your hands messing things up, NOT HIS!

This was a very true statement, so now I dream BIG! I reach for my goals in life, plans for my family. I don't limit Him in my life. I live every day seeing that He will use me somehow to make a difference in this world; I see his blessing and favor all around me. Now I am not saying that my life is all rainbows and bursts of sunshine all the time. I have my moments of struggles; we have setbacks like everyone else. But for the most part, He continues to show up in my family's life and works in our hearts.

I want you to ask yourself this question: "What do you want to do when you get clean and sober?"

Go back to school? Start a career? Start a business? Start a family? Rebuild? What is it? Whatever it is, you can do it. Right now, I want you to start thinking positively! No matter how life is looking for you right now, you need to get that positive spirit back in your thoughts, heart, and mind. Know that even though things look bad right now, God can turn it all around for good! He wants to bless you. He wants to restore you; He wants to see you succeed. You may have put the pen down to stop writing your story, pick it back up again. It is not done yet.

But while you are reading this, you have to believe it. You have to see good in all the bad. See good amid the struggles; you have to see the light in all the darkness. If someone had told me 11 years ago what I would be doing today, I promise I wouldn't believe it in my low times of addiction. If someone said I would be writing a book or trying to get a detox home going, I wouldn't believe it. But here I am now, and you and I are not any different. It's the drive that people have. It has that attitude that enough is enough; we have been doing this for too long, and things need to change. We deserve a good life. Our families deserve a good life. Your heart just has to be willing, your spirit needs to be positive, and your mind needs to keep sharp.

As long as you say: "My life will always be this way," it will be. As long as you say: "I am never going to get clean and sober," you won't. As long as you keep spinning your mind in being defeatist and waiting for bad things to happen, they will. I am not sharing my life with you to say: "Look at me," but to show you a NEW way of thinking. If God can use me, He can use anyone. If He can turn my life around, He can do the same for you too. Move forward and tell yourself you deserve a good life. You deserve good things! I hope you will write me and let me know what you are doing now and how God uses you. The sky is the limit for you, friend. Get going! Think positive! See good!

Much love,
Anthony Torres

"If this number of only 10% don't receive treatment doesn't bother you, it should. This means only 10% or less actually start to clean up their lives"

LETTER 34

THOUGHTS ABOUT
'10%'

Almost 21 million Americans have at least one addiction, yet only 10% of them receive treatment.
Not sure what state you live in, but in New Mexico, according to the NM Department Of Health every 18 hours, someone dies of an overdose.

Since I have been in ministry, I have said prayers over many people whose lives are about to be cut short due to an overdose. The only thing keeping them alive is the ventilator, and there is nothing more the doctors can do. There I am, holding hands with the family in a circle, feeling the damp, sweaty hands of a mother because she has been up at the hospital for days believing for a miracle for their son or daughter. As we pray one last time over their loved ones, the doctors come in and begin to take them off the machine. Now, all I can hear is the sounds of sniffles, and I see tears running down faces. This will always be in my mind forever. This is the moment they are about to take their last breath on earth; a life cut short by addiction is now in the hands of the good Lord.

But what will always get me and still stays with me to this day is when the doctors come in and start unhooking them off the machine. All you hear is the screams of a mother, or in one case, a son hovering over his mom's body crying, saying, "I love you, mommy." With every minute that passes, their breaths become more shallow. The doctors turn off the heart monitor, so the family can't see the heartbeat go down, and within minutes passing, their breathing is becoming more shallow, they cry, and sniffles of the family become more intense. At that moment, all I can do is pray and ask God to be with this family as I have tears running down my face as well, then just like that, the doctors call the time of death. And another brother or sister loses their life to addiction. That could have been me; it could have been you. As I type this thought right now, we lost another brother or sister due to addiction in the world somewhere.

How many times did I stick my fingers down my throat to vomit because I was afraid I did too much cocaine, mixed with pills, too many shots, too much beer, and I felt like my whole body was going to shut down, then after I vomited, I turned around to use again? How many nights did I run the water over my face because I felt like I would pass out and die? One night I swore I would not wake up the following day. Or how many times did I stare down a barrel of a gun because I wanted out so bad? My addiction kept me down for too long, and you can't let it keep you either. The numbers of addiction are alarming, and they seem never to get better as the years go on. You see younger people now adding to the number of overdoses.

Only 10% of people get help in their recovery; why is that? Pride? Ego? Or do they just worry about what people will say or think if they clean up their lives? Let me ask this clearly, WHO CARES WHAT PEOPLE THINK?! It would be best if you got better for yourself and your family.

Are we also not providing enough programs or resources for people to get help? It can be several things. If you are reading this book right now, I encourage you to find a program, faith-based or secular, classes or a group you can be a part of. You need some tools to help set you free from this addiction.

If this number of only 10% don't receive treatment doesn't bother you, it should. This means only 10% or less actually start to clean up their lives. We live in a world where we spin our wheels in addiction and then wonder why we are 60 years old still dealing with this in our lives. I don't know about you, friend, but I just didn't want some things to change in my life. I wanted ALL things to change in my life. Now I am not saying that I am perfect, it's been 11 years, and I am still working on myself. But I can say this with complete confidence that I am not the same man I was in 2009. I may still battle sometimes and war within my mind and spirit, but I don't do it alone anymore. I have Christ in my life now. He helps me with those battles within my head. My soul can no longer scream out and cry within and say: "no more," He gives me His spirit and word that things are going to be okay.

See, back then, those battles were fought in the room with my bottle, my anger, my drugs, my suicidal thoughts. Every hit, every drink silenced the voices in my head. And for that moment, it was silent in my soul. It was like for once nothing in that room mattered; I was at peace. But I can't battle like that anymore, and neither can you. That war, that battle in our minds, is real, and I believe it is spiritual. Trust me when I say that I had too many of those nights. I didn't know if I would come out of it alive during some of those nights if you know what I mean.

This is why we need something in our lives to help us, to help us heal, rebuild, and feel alive again.

I genuinely believe that we have many people just coping with things and life, just getting by. That's why relapse happens so much in a person's life, and no breakthrough ever comes. They spend their whole life barely coping with things instead of coming to a place of complete restoration, a place of total healing for their lives. Stop managing and start healing!

I'm sure you've heard the word "HEALING" a lot, and you're probably thinking, what do you mean by total healing? I mean healing from past hurts, past regrets, past abuse, past pain, past trauma. Things that keep us stuck and don't allow us to move forward. I understand it will take some time to get to a complete healing place, and I am not talking about over-night healing. But we can't just cope with it and deal with it. Let's find healthy ways to overcome these areas in our lives, which is also essential in our recovery.

The purpose of this thought is to seek treatment, a pro-gram, a rehab, something that is going to teach you a different way, an alternative to what you have been doing. Once you learn, apply it to your life. If you are a Christian, your bible is a good start for you. I started reading it in rehab, and it began to touch the depth of my soul before I got out and started to use drugs again. I wasn't strong enough, and once again, the addiction overshadowed what I was reading.

I am not sure what it looks like for you to get in that 10%, but for me, it's Jesus! He is my rehab, every day, every minute of my life. This is not a famous saying nor popular teaching. But you have to understand this is all I know. When I was at my lowest, rock bottom lowest, I cried out to God; I cried out to be saved from this hell of an addiction and the demons who tormented me. He showed me who He was after cussing at him and denying him for years.

Now, this is my journey, and I understand that not every-one's journey is like mine. The only picture I can give you is that of Lt. Dan Taylor from the movie *Forrest Gump*. When they were at sea, and a storm came, Lt. Dan was on the high end of the pole cussing at God as the storm raged. He was letting out everything he had inside of him, every battle, every struggle;

he EMPTIED himself till he had no more inside to give. And like Forrest said after the storm was over, he believed. Lt. Dan made peace with God that day.

That was me on the day I made peace with myself. For once, I was at peace with God. I had emptied myself, and all He could do was fill me up with him. And for once, I was exposed/naked, to the point where I said: "HERE I AM," because I knew I needed something new in my life. Sometimes in this awful life, all we need is to make our peace with God daily, even if we don't have peace with people. I believe it will be his peace that will sustain us.

As I write this, friend, many are choosing to stay in their addiction. Many are choosing not to change, choosing not to seek some help. Have you had enough in your life that you have done? Are you truly done with living this life of addiction? I started this thought with a person dying from an overdose because I want you to think about your life as precious and promising.

I can categorically say that I have seen many people come out of it, and they do nothing with that second chance, that third or fourth chance of life they were given. They go right back to prison or go back to drugs after coming out of a coma. I didn't want to be remembered for that. I wanted to be remembered for having tried every day to get better. I tried every day to overcome this addiction. I tried every day to let God handle the battle in my mind, heart, and spirit. I am not saying it's easy; what I am saying is it will be worth it. Stay in it and seek help.

How bad do you want it? How bad do you want to stop using drugs and alcohol? How badly do you want to stop doing this battle alone? A struggle that has become too much for you to bear. If you are reading this, it's your time to shine! It is your time to overcome! It is definitely your time to live again!

It's your time to stop doing these battles alone! It is time! I want you to be in that 10%. Let's go!

Much love,
Anthony Torres

https://www.addictioncenter.com/addiction/addiction-statistics/
https://www.nmhealth.org/publication/view/marketing/2117/

"Recovery is not meant to be easy,

or else everyone would be doing it"

LETTER 35

THOUGHTS ABOUT
'TRUST THE PROCESS'

I f there is one thing that you and I don't like, it is waiting. McDonald's now has two lines instead of one, and there is a reason for this, we get impatient. It's called fast food for a reason. If we have to wait longer than we think it should take, we naturally get very impatient. For example, on our cell phones, we now have 5G connectivity but still get upset when we get no service. We laugh at this, but we know that it is true. We naturally do not like to be kept waiting.

Here are some words you may not want to hear: Whether you like it or not, you will have to wait and trust your recovery process; it could be months or even years. You might shut my book after reading this, but your recovery is not on your terms or demands; it is in whatever it looks like to get clean and sober. Listen, I have been doing this long enough that I can talk to someone over the phone or sit with them in my office, and within a few moments of our conversation, I can tell if they want to get clean and sober. In most of the cases, they set up this appointment with me of their own volition, or they speak to me because it will look good when they talk to their PO (probation officer), or their wives or husbands told them that if they didn't seek help, they would divorce them. They are in my office for all the wrong reasons, and I quickly pick up on that.

You might ask how I know this; it is simply because it's not them listening to me. It is them telling me how they want their recovery to go, telling me what they want, or that they will only get help IF things happen on their terms. It becomes a one-sided conversation, and I start to see that their recovery is based on what they want instead of what they need to get help.

Most of the time, the conversations go like this: "I love my boyfriend too much to be apart from him for so long, I can't leave him," or "6 months is too long for me to be away, I need to work."

Okay, I get it! But you're far away in your mind with drugs and alcohol anyway, and you're hurting everyone you love, you are hurting yourself every day that you put it off, you're digging for yourself a deeper hole trying to get sober and clean on your terms. So what are six months to a year going to do to you? Is it going to kill you? Compared to the effects of your addiction?

In your recovery, you will be stretched and challenged. You will be out of your comfort zone. You will be in an unfamiliar place and put in environments that you never thought you would find yourself. But whatever program you go with, four months to a year is suitable for your well-being and whatever plan you set in place.

Another question I get a lot is, "Can I just do 30 days? I think that will be a better program for me." Now, let's consider this logically, you have been doing hard drugs for 2-10 years, and you think a 30-day program is going to help? You have been drinking since you were 15, and now you're 30 or 40 looking to get sober, and 30 days is going to be enough? I really am not trying to be a negative person here, but it will take more than 30 days.

We need to deal with many learned behaviors. There are many bad habits we need to address, a lot of wrong thinking we need to work out. Soul searching is the key! Learning to get through things in whatever life throws at you will be so crucial in your recovery.

So think of it like this, If you squeeze an orange. What do you get? Orange Juice.

Addicted or not, life will come at you in every direction you can think of; it will try to destroy you and get you to quit. It will squeeze you. But what is going to come out of you? Your old or new ways? Old thinking or new? Do you get what I am saying?

A life in recovery is a new way of living. And this is where you have to trust the process.

My friend, we haven't even scratched the surface yet in the process of recovery. We are just barely getting started. Now I am not dismissing that you can turn this around in 30 days; it can happen, but have you developed the skills to overcome it? To heal! Remember we talked about that in one of my thoughts. You want to make sure you have the tools in your bag to use when the pressures of life come. With this, you won't go back to your addiction. Believe me; I would be lying if I said that I never had thoughts of going back to my old life every time things got hard. I had to put to work all the things I have learned over the years to have come this far. And thankfully, I have God on my side.

Thirty days is not enough time to dig up your roots and learn. This is why it is so essential to trust the process. Fathers listen; I know you have to work to provide for your kids; I know a long-term program might not work. But it will be the BEST time to find YOU, get out, and be sober and clean. It will be the best time to be fresh and look through the eyes of sobriety over addiction and defeat. Think about it like this; we spend more time chasing drugs and getting high in a year.

Most of the time, we will be out of our comfort zone, and sometimes that is a good place if you choose a rehab. But whatever you decide to get better, trust the process.

Mothers, I know this thought is complex for you also because you're thinking, "Who is going to watch my kids while I am gone?" "Who is going to be there for them?" Going to a rehab center is more challenging for a mother than a father because right away, they are thinking: "Who will take care of them?" Who is going to nurse and feed them? You are always in the 'momma' mode, and I understand that.

But think about how strong and more valuable you will be to your kids if you got sober and clean. Think about how much energy you will have, how much clarity you will get. Like I told the fathers, you will be out of your comfort zone, and you will be stretched. Whatever plan you choose, stick with it and trust the process.

But let's find the help that we need for ourselves. Four months to a year is not a death sentence for a recovery program or whatever plan you pick to get sober and clean.

I believe that you get what you put in recovery. Quickly, I want to touch on these three points in trusting the process.

Commit

Whatever program, short or long term, please commit to it. You have to make up your mind that no matter how hard it gets, how uncomfortable you get, or how uneasy you're going to get, you need to commit to this program, ride it out! Learn to trust the process. You're in a place with different personalities, different backgrounds, and attitudes. But everyone is there for a purpose. To get clean and sober, learn new teachings and ways of life. Stick it out and be committed; give room for a chance before you make that phone call for someone to get you. Be committed to anything that you are doing to get better.

It will be beneficial for you. Recovery is not meant to be easy, or else everyone would be doing it. Where ever you are at, give it a shot and stay in it. If it is not a rehab, maybe it's classes or a group. It could be counseling; make sure you put that on your schedule and prioritize it daily and weekly. Commitment is not going to be a short time thing; it will be long-term.

Submit

Submit to your teachers or leaders. Listen to their teachings. One hundred percent of the time, the person teaching or trying to help you is someone that has been in your shoes, someone that has gone through the same battles as you have. Submit to the teachings and allow them to be a part of your life, take what you can, and apply them. It's not like they are telling you something that will harm you; it will help, encourage and build you up.

To walk into a program with the mindset that you're not going to listen to anything, and you're just going to do your thing, do your time, and get out, is as though setting yourself up to fail. Bring a notepad to this program, listen and apply it to your life. If there is something that I have applied to my life today, it will always be wanting to be a student—both in my recovery, ministry, and life. When we think we know it all and are not teachable, we find ourselves in trouble quickly. When we want always to be the teacher, we will never learn.

I have seen a lot of bad attitudes when it comes to learning over the years. Submitting and being a student in recovery and life is a good thing. By doing this, we set ourselves up for success.

Learn

You have to be like a sponge in these programs or groups, learn what you can. Unlearn what you need to. Learn to get through your triggers, to overcome depression and anxiety. Learn about your addiction, learn about you, to be happy for once. Learn to do good! There is so much in your recovery to learn.

For me, it was reading my bible and learning about God, learning about me, all over again. I was no longer the Anthony a few years ago. I was someone new. I had to learn different things about myself, learn new ways to love others, and recover. But pay attention and learn as much as you can. So when you get out, you can apply everything you have learned to your new life in recovery.

Do you know what these three points have in common? We were COMMITTED to our drugs in our addiction, we SUBMITTED to alcohol, and LEARNED a life of addiction.

Here is a question before we end: If we can do all these things in addiction. How come we can't do these things in our recovery? It is a lot to think about, I know.

I always tell people I was sold out for my high, for my drink, for my darkness. I didn't care who I hurt or what I did. I wanted my addiction more than anything in life. I was sold-out for it, sold out for the lifestyle I lived for so many years.

Why not be that way in your recovery?! As a pastor in my church, I am always working on projects for the community and our church. I have a lot of people that tell me, "You need to slow down," "You do too much."

Maybe so! But they don't know how sold out I was for addiction. I want to be sold out for my recovery, for my God, and my purpose. That way, when I die and leave this earth, I can say I gave everything I had. I pray that you get the desire to do the same in your life.

So COMMIT, SUBMIT, and LEARN!

Remember, If you really want to get sober and clean, it will not be on your terms. It's going to be in your program for recovery. Trust the process, don't give up too soon! Your blessing and breakthrough are right around the corner.

Much Love,
Anthony Torres

"When the Christian RELAPSES

"I feel you all around me, But do you want any part of me?"
At that moment, I seek temporary peace, with every smoke,
every snort of Cocaine, Every vein jabbed with heroin, Every
drink. I have relapsed! Am I this weak?

I can't feel you anymore! Have I disgusted you? This darkness is around me, through me, is it for me? I can feel the ra-
zor blades of the high cutting me up inside. Will you hear me
if I cry? I'm trying every day. But sometimes I think I will always be this way?

Then suddenly, the clouds begin to break. The sun shines
again, not the sun of the earth. But the SON of my soul, the
SON of God. I can feel him like a rushing wind; he rescues
me, he reassures me of his eternal LOVE. Then it's in that moment I realize I am HIS

"Identify and work through those

triggers"

LETTER 36

THOUGHTS ABOUT
'TRIGGERS'

W hile in Oklahoma in 2009, it had been some days since I had any alcohol and drugs in my system. I felt for once that I was making a turnaround in my life. I felt good most days; I was alone most of the time. On some days, my depression would hit me heavy out of the blue, but I pressed through, I would have sleepless nights every once in a while. On some days, I would walk the reservoir during the day and look at the calm waters and think to myself for some time; I reflected a lot on my life. I had many questions for myself. Like can I really live a sober and clean life? What would my life look like?

I enjoyed going to Church to hear Pastor Lopez preach and listen to what God put in his heart. Going to church was something new to me, but I am glad I stuck with it. Church life was very new to me. As I write this, I miss him terribly. He believed in me. He would encourage me and pray for me. He always made me feel welcome; he never looked down on me. Even in times he knew I wasn't doing good, he never judged me. To hear his voice and to listen to him say: "Brother Anthony, you're going to be okay" would mean the world to me.

But most days, when I let my emotions get the best of me, I always felt trapped. I don't know if that makes any sense.

233

When that urge to use drugs or drink would come up, I would read my word, pray and ask God to help me like Pastor Lopez had taught me to do—but missing my kids, trying to deal with every bit of emotion soberly, ensuring that every thought was clean? It happens very quickly, and as expected, one day I broke!

I gave in to my triggers, and I walked to the store and got myself a 40 oz of Bud light. I drank and called someone I met in Altus to get me a 60 worth of coke, and boom, I was on a binge again. Then I begin to wrestle with my heart if God was truly with me. I questioned what I was doing wrong. Thankfully in those times, Pastor Lopez was there to walk it through with me.

But what do we do with our triggers? This is the purpose for which I'm sharing this thought with you. Those triggers will come in full force like a hurricane, so we need to know how to work through them when they arrive. I didn't even know what that meant back then like I do now. I just gave in to what I felt at the moment, and then I would relapse because it was so easy. Giving in to our addictions is the easy part; working through them is the discipline part.

Have you gotten to the point where you feel your triggers coming? Or you know something that will set you off? What are you going to do?

A lady once told me that her being alone was her trigger; she hated it. So she would drink to pass out so as not to feel alone. One guy said when he would hear threats and negative words from his baby's momma to keep the kids from seeing him, how she would yell at him that he was a "Dead Beat Dad" triggered him.

You see, every one of us has different triggers that we have to navigate through. Your first year will be the hardest, but as more time of being clean and sober passes, you will have a handle on your triggers, and they won't have a hold on you anymore. The reality is every person, addicted or not, has triggers; it is what we do at that moment that will make all the difference in recovery.

Even today, being clean and sober, I still have triggers, but I have learned over the years not to go back to old habits and to think like I used to. So here we go. The first thing I learned is:

Identifying your Triggers

Identify what is keeping you grounded in your addiction; is it your thoughts? Is it your environment? Is it the people you are hanging around with? Once you can pinpoint this, you can navigate them. However, there are some things you can't avoid (such as what people say or how they treat you), but you can constantly adjust.

I will give you some of mine; maybe they will be the same for you, perhaps they won't. This will look very different for you as we all come from different backgrounds with diverse cultures.

One of my triggers was being **alone**! I found out very quickly that I did not like to be alone. The more I was alone, the more I thought about using, the more I got caught up in my own emotions. The more I felt like I needed to keep myself entertained. When this would happen, I would call someone on the phone or start a conversation in my space or go out to eat or watch a movie. Sometimes, I will go for a walk or to the gym; the point is I kept going. I never let my mind go idle, and I wouldn't attempt to lay on the couch. I kept going! I'm going to be forty in 20 days, so I am okay with being alone now. But in my recovery, it was my trigger. Find a good friend, if you can, to walk this journey with you. I eventually found a friend

I could call to eat or to a movie or just hang out. I was thankful for those friendships during my recovery.

The other one was **Stress.** Everyone in the world deals with stress. I even dealt with it today. The kind of stress that I am talking about is, nothing is going your way, sort of pressure. You get up every day and put in work, and nothing is working. Your kids don't want to hear from you; all those doors you thought were opening back up to get on your feet have shut. You made three steps forward, and one day, you wake up five steps backward. It's a season where you see nothing going your way. It can be really stressful, where waking up every day is a struggle.

What can happen in moments like this is we say: "I guess I was never meant to have a good life" or "this is hard work, what is the point?" Let me touch on this thought for a second.

It is not just going to be about you getting up and putting in work; you might have to put in overtime. Did we think 10-20 years of addiction was going to turn into weeks worth of easy work in getting on our feet? The easy part is going back to drinking, going back to drugs, and the hard part is sticking with it! The hard part is working through the stress. I have said it many times. You think life is tough, try doing it "clean and sober," but guess what? Even today, we all deal with stress when things are not going our way. What I started doing was journaling, going to the gym, going for a walk at dawn. I read many books, and I read my bible. I went to church or bible studies. Times that I would just lie on the couch with my forearm over my head and take deep breaths to pray.

I found new and healthy ways to deal with stress because I found out that in life, some things will never go our way, and things change so fast. I wrote this book during a pandemic called Covid-19. 2020 was a year of loss, adjustments, days of the unknown, and even days of death.

But what it also taught me and those in recovery is that we can adjust; we have the strength to adapt if we want to. You see, the problem we have is we don't like change, good or bad. We feel that we would be okay if things never change, so things just stayed the same. But Covid-19 proved there will always be something to challenge us as people. People had to dig deep in their hearts to see what they were made of; we had to see what areas in our lives we needed to work on and how much we trust God like we say we do. This is you in your recovery; right now, you are being challenged; you see what you are made of in times of adversity. But listen to me when I say you have the ability to adjust and the strength to adapt in your recovery. You can dig deep into your own heart and see what you are made of. That was how it was for me; it was a time I needed to trust God more in my life. So we need to deal with that stress healthily. Sadly in life, things never go our way, but we do the best that we can.

My **past** was another one. Your past is something that you and I can never get back; we love to revisit it, don't we? And we mustn't stay there for too long. You have to let go and keep your eyes on the present. The past is like pouring acid on your eyes; it blinds you to what your life is becoming in your recovery (Good) vs. what you are looking back at (Bad). But what helped me was ONE, God forgave me, and TWO, I was seeing all the progress I was making. Get past these thoughts quickly, or you will stay in your mind too long, and you could find yourself going back to your addiction. You heard that saying on why we have rearview mirrors when we drive? It is so that we can look at the road behind us while we go forward. This is the same in recovery; when you are moving a bus forward in recovery, why look back? Why are you stopping to pick up and entertain thoughts that keep you stuck? Why? We talked about it in "Reflection in the mirror"; forgiveness is a must. When we spend time in the past, we open up old wounds and bleed on everything that was forgiven by God again. Why are we now trying to get back to that place by spending time in the past? Well, you can spend as much time as you want in the past, but I assure you, it won't help you get to your future. Wash your eyes, get that acid out and keep focused. Don't let this trigger keep you too long because it can, and it will if you allow it. Remember, living in the past won't let you enjoy the present.

The last one is **Cravings**. The smell and taste of drugs and alcohol will drive us crazy if we let it at the start of our recovery. We will claw and scratch up a wall to get a taste of being high again if we don't get this in check. What I did early into my recovery, which still sounds ridiculous, is that I got rid of all my bud light posters, shirts, and hats—anything with an alcohol emblem I tossed in the trash. I avoided the sugar and liquor aisle at the grocery store for a while. I made no eye contact with the white powdered sugar, which would make my mind wander to see the liquor. I could smell and even taste the "Jack Daniels" on the gums of my teeth. I avoided those areas like the plague. That sounds so silly, but I didn't want any of my cravings to come up. But when they did, I drank coffee. I watched a movie to get my mind off it. Maybe I would drink a Dr. Pepper! I pop some gummies bears in my mouth or get ice cream. Call a friend for prayer at times too. Please do what you need to do in a healthy way to pass through these cravings because they will come. One time, I began to cook for no reason. I did what I needed to do to take my mind off my cravings. This was a physical need for my body, but I needed to give it good stuff. I needed to push back those feelings of needing or wanting the old stuff in my body. Cravings are real, and they can be brutal sometimes. But we have to do what we need to, so we don't give in to that moment of cravings.

One day I thought my tattoos would come off, from me digging my nails into my skin because that craving was intense and overwhelming. But here is the encouraging part, once you get past those cravings, it becomes gradually easy, until one day, where you won't have those cravings anymore.

Here is something I try to do daily: "Starve the flesh, feed the spirit". What does this mean? We all have a spirit. When the spirit is strong, we don't give in to what the flesh wants. Does this make sense? I believed in my heart that Christ helped me with mine in those moments. Alcohol was my biggest weakness, and I thought for sure I was going to die an alcoholic. But after a while, after praying and really just crying out to God to help me, after doing what I needed to do to get by those days and nights, my cravings went away!

My biggest struggle today is now doughnuts or fruit, Big Mac, or chicken with rice! Go to the gym or no gym. But I think I am getting better in these areas. At least I think I do, but my wife might not think so.

I hope some of this helped you. Triggers will look different for you. Once, someone told me that his trigger was a certain cologne he would smell. If he sensed it, he was reminded of that abusive relationship he once had because the abuser wore the cologne often. It brought back a lot of old memories and hurt to his life. When this happens, he felt the need to use drugs to numb the pain and drink to forget that memory.

But your job after this thought is to IDENTIFY and work through those triggers. Remember, it will require work, backbreaking labor for you in your spirit, but you can and will do it. I know you can. This is the hard part for all of us in recovery; getting past the triggers.

Triggers come daily for everyone. It is always finding new ways to deal with us. But you're not alone in this, friend. You can do this! I am cheering you on all the way from New Mexico. Today, I hope and pray your triggers don't break you but rather make you stronger in life, and in your journey to recovery, I leave you with this last thought: It is easy to give in to those triggers, but it will take real discipline in your life to not. Discipline yourself, friends.

Much love,
Anthony Torres

"You have to replace 'bad' talk

with 'good' talk for your life in

recovery"

LETTER 37

THOUGHTS ABOUT
'REPLACE'

I was going on months being sober and clean, I was angry, and I was dealing with emotions that I had never felt before; there were days I was grumpy for no reason. It was like my body was trying to get used to not having any toxins in it. It was at a place that I have never been before in my sobriety. My friend, you are on a new level when you start doing life sober and clean; you are not burying your emotions anymore and trying to forget them. You're not masking your pain anymore, and you are not numbing life! You now deal with it head-on. You try to do your best to deal with life with a clear mind now.

Replace!

A word I'm going to use in this thought because it's a significant one. Think of yourself on a boat in the ocean in the middle of a storm, and you're drunk. What are you more likely to do? Keep drinking because you are afraid or maybe not? Know now that nothing on that boat won't get to you emotionally. You will have what we call "Liquid courage." You won't be living in fear of dying on that boat. The alcohol will numb any thoughts you have, your mind will wander off, and if you die, you die.

Now let's play the same scenario, but you're not drunk this time, but scared to your wits. You are screaming for help, and help won't come for another 2 hours. You can't help but think for a second, all these bad things: "Do I want to die?" "Will someone come and rescue me?" "Will I see dry land again?" "What are we going to do?"

See, this storm is your life, and it is my life. The boat is our safe place; it is what we created. When we are drunk or high, we don't care if we sink. When we are sober and clean in that boat, we are just trying to stay afloat—hanging on to another day.

In your recovery, you have to replace your old thinking with NEW ones. Life will continue to come after you and me, but we can't go back to our old thinking. We can't go back to our old ways. Your thought right now is probably this: "How can I get over this trial in my life without going back to drinking or doing drugs?" Instead, this is what we need to say: "I can't see my kids right now, but I won't let this discourage me." "Everyone has turned their backs on me, but I will press through." "My ex is not making my life any easier with the negative comments toward me, but that's not me anymore." "I am having a hard time finding a job and getting back on my feet, but something will open up."

You have to be your biggest voice in times of pain and difficulties, seasons where days just don't go our way. You have to accept the good and the bad of life in your Recovery class. We always start the class with highs and lows. Highs are good things that are happening in life right now, such as: "I just got a job, or I can now talk to my kids," lows are things that just didn't go our way, such as struggling to find a job or getting fired.

In my observation, people who relapse have been discouraged. So, I try to teach the men and women that they have to

244

learn to accept the good and bad in recovery. Sometimes it is not balanced, and that's okay. There were many times I had to look at myself in the mirror and say, "It's been months! You can't go back now; keep moving", "I don't have a job, but one day I will", or "I don't like staying at my mom's house, but one day I will have my own place."

You see? You have to replace 'bad' talk with 'good' talk for your life in recovery.

Talk to someone if you can or to your journal where you don't have someone to talk to. I journaled a lot in my recovery time because I needed to get all those thoughts out of my head and put positive ones on paper. I had to replace my old thoughts with new ones.

You also have to replace bad habits with healthy habits. We were so notorious due to our bad habits; that's what got most of us in trouble from the very beginning. We usually don't have a problem creating bad habits; that comes easy to us—but creating new habits? That can be challenging, but we can do it.

I knew that I could eventually kick the drugs, but I knew that drinking would be hard for me, but I kept going regardless. On one of those horrible days, I was itching to go to the store and grab a beer. As I was driving around, trying to figure out what I was going to do, I pulled up at the park of a convenience store and watched men and women come out of the store with liquor and beer. My mind began to wonder; it was like a movie, but I knew what would happen if I gave in to my trigger. I thought to myself: "What would my family think?" "Would Sasha leave me again?" Giving in is the easy part. The ability to not go through with it is a struggle. As I sat there: I bit my bottom lip almost till it bled, and my hands squeezed the steering wheel so tightly I had cramps in my hands. I turned on worship music and begun to sing from the top of my lungs. I thought about how much progress I was making in my recovery. So I punched the steering wheel and went to get some food; the Burger dripping with grease, pickles, and mustard loaded with bacon won the battle that day against me giving in to my drinking, and I was okay with that. Sometimes, the best thing to do is to drive away and not look back. Fortunately, I survived another day, but I would have been three months to a year down the drain if I had gone through with it.

Now I'm not asking you to replace burgers with beer every time you get an itch!

All I'm saying is that you have to fight that urge to go down that old adverse road that you no longer tread anymore. Instead, it would be best to replace that with positive thoughts of how far you have come and what your life can look like by being sober and clean. Remember, your voice has to be louder and bigger than your addictions. No one is going to change this for you. You own your mind. The ball is in your court.

The other thing I want to talk about is to Replace your bad attitude with a positive one. You may not like where you are in your life right now, but this is where you are at due to your addictions. Consider a situation where you have a new way of **THINKING**, **TALKING**, and a new **ATTITUDE;** how great will you feel inside?

There is no sense in making a situation seem more profound than it is. I knew in my heart that I would not be staying in my aunt's house forever in Oklahoma. I knew that I wasn't going to be alone forever; I knew one day I would have a job and take care of myself and my kids again. I hoped for one day to be a family man again. I knew walking around and riding a bicycle to get me where I needed to go was not going to be forever; one day, I would have a car I can call mine. Did I like where I was at that moment? Of course not. I saw it as a time to rebuild my life, a time to put the pieces back together for the brokenness that I had created and do this life the right way for once. With my new-found faith, I felt more potent than ever.

I looked at life a little differently. It didn't matter how bad things looked or felt for me. I had to change and replace my perspective with a good attitude, good talk, and habits. We give in to our destructive emotions too much in life. It is time we start letting the positive ones lead us.

This is what you will do. You may not like being in prison, rehab, away from your family, sleeping on different couches, or on the streets! You may not be happy that you don't even have a dollar to get something from the menu at Burger King or money to buy your kids a gift for Christmas or even their birthday. But this won't be forever! As you move forward and put in work every day, replaced with a positive outlook and a positive attitude, things will begin to fall in place. Don't forget: this will definitely take some time.

If you can apply these things that I have shared with you to your life, I assure you that you will see changes in how your heart and mind are wired and, consequently, how you view your recovery. But if you're going to be negative all the time to the point that all that comes out of your mouth is doubt, disbelief, and negative words in any and every situation you find yourself in, your journey to recovery is going to be miserable. You're going to start to believe your own lies and drown in them. And if this continues, there is a high chance that you would relapse. There is a chance that you would start to get stuck. Please don't do it, friend! Listen, nobody owes you anything. You owe yourself that luxury of RECOVERY as well as a better version of yourself.

So remember, you need to REPLACE your old thinking with new thinking, a new voice instead of an old one, and a good attitude over a bad one. Your voice has to be bigger than any negative thought you have about yourself or even about life in any season you find yourself. Notwithstanding what life decides to put you through, you have to accept the good and the bad to recover! It's a must! Don't let this discourage you, friends.

Much love,
Anthony Torres

"Your consistency is the key in your recovery process, not your words"

LETTER 38

Thoughts about
'Trust that Hurts'

If there are words that recovering addicts don't like to hear when we are working hard in our recovery, they are "You're drinking again, aren't you?" or "Are you High Again?" or "You've been cheating again, haven't you?" These words hurt so much, especially when we know deep down in our spirits that we haven't been doing any of those. For once in our lives, we are walking a straight line and doing good.

I think one of my biggest challenges in life was gaining back the trust of my family. Sasha and I spent many days climbing that mountain together when it came to trust. We had spent enough time in the valley (hardships), we needed to hold hands and do this together.

People look at her now and think she has it all together. But if only you knew what I had put this beautiful woman through emotionally, you would ask yourself, "Why is she even still with him?" When you tear down someone for so long, when you belittle them, when you take their voice away, it's hard to begin to help build them back up, to make them feel important again. Lord knew I had a lot of work to do in building her trust back.

God knows that I have so many regrets in life, cheating on her and lying is one of them. My life back then was drugs, girls, alcohol, and my motorcycle. It's like I was leading a double life. I did it for so long to the point that I didn't even know who I was anymore. I got lost in the midst of that and I was having a very hard time finding my way back. The smoke was too thick, the clouds were getting too dark for me to find my way back. I had no guide nor direction.

Betrayal can hurt and run deep in our hearts and be piercing to our skin. Especially if it's from those we love and trust! Our spouse once believed in us, didn't they? They fell in love with us for a reason, they had our kids or we had theirs because we knew what love and family meant to us. But now what we say doesn't matter to them.

How many times have our loved ones heard, "I won't drink anymore, I won't use drugs anymore, I will stay out of prison, jail and trouble this time. I promise things will be different. Give me a chance. I am TELLING THE TRUTH this time," and then we back it up with our famous words of "I PROMISE."

Do you remember the teacher in Charlie Brown? Every time she spoke, it was WHA, WHA, WHA. I think this is how we sound to our families every time we say "I won't" or "I promise." I want you to let these words go deep into your heart.

Your consistency is the key in your recovery process, not your words.

So, in other words, what matters is your actions and how many times you do them, not what you say.

Our families have heard all the excuses in the world, promise after promise. But what they want is to see you DO, not SPEAK! I'm not saying this to make you feel bad, friend. I'm saying this just to make a point. This is something I had to learn very quickly on my road to recovery. When Sasha and I got back together, I had to do things differently, because one sign of me using again, one act of me going back to my old ways, I knew she would leave me again, and this time, she wasn't going to come back. I didn't want that.

On Saturdays, I would get up at 5:30am to get ready for Bible study. Sasha was in shock when she would hear my alarm go off for me to get up. Back in the day, I was usually coming home at this time from being out all night, or still up from a day's binge.

However, nobody had to tell me to get better, it was deep in my heart. Nobody had to make me go to classes or Bible studies, I went because I needed it. Not for anyone else, but for me. I was sick and tired of my empty life. I found a new one filled with joy and promises. I was on a new level in life. I think talking helps us to identify what we need to do in our lives, so we should voice it out loud to our family - just say it. Even so, we have to be careful what we say and what we do here on out.

In this thought, I want to give you some things that will help you regain the trust of your spouse, your family and your loved ones. But listen to me when I say it will take some time. And you can't get frustrated with the process.

Here we go.

Being Consistent is the KEY

Being consistent with our actions and promises will help us to establish trust again with our family and they will see a good PATTERN. Instead of a pattern of broken promises or destructive behaviors, they will see new ones and new promises. This will get their attention, believe it or not. Something will "Ding" in their minds like "Maybe he or she really wants to change." But I am not talking about a couple of days, or a few weeks. I am talking about months. I looked back in my life and saw that I could go two weeks without using, but then something always came up, and there I was again back in my puddle of mess. Having months of a good pattern is a big challenge. But it's something I know that you can do.

If you have to go to group, do it. If you have to go to church, then go. If it's your weekend to pick up your kids, then pick them up. Whatever it is, make sure you're consistent with it. For me, it was Church. This was something new to me and my family. My family knew that on Sundays, we were going to church. Every time those church doors opened, we were there.

I enjoyed my men's bible study. Most importantly, I enjoyed getting to know the new me. I kept on doing what I needed to do to stay clean and sober, nobody had to tell me. I just did it!

And listen, I am not saying a week of doing this then we sit back and expect results. No! Just keep doing it, it could take weeks, maybe even months. And you have to understand why you're doing it. But don't get discouraged if you don't get a pat on the back or see instant praise from your family. Show your family and loved ones you're setting new priorities in your life, and nothing is going to get in the way of this. Be consistent!

Don't talk, just do it

Don't say you're going to do better, just do it! Don't say this is the last time I am out of prison or rehab. Just stay out! Don't say I am going to be a better person, just be better!

I realized I had made a lot of broken promises I couldn't keep. I didn't want to start building those false hopes again and then let them down. So I just kept my mouth shut and did it. I knew I wanted a better future with my family. I didn't talk, I just did what I needed to do to position ourselves to be along further every year than we were before, to be together, to be healthy as a family.

I knew that one day I wanted to be years and years clean and sober, so I did what I needed to do to position myself to be that, and to WIN! I was tired of feeling like a loser, tired of letting everyone down. I was tired of making a mess of everything. So I didn't talk, I just did! I knew I needed to be more loving, more caring. I just did it. At least, I tried. Highlight this: Action is better than words, and doing is better than making promises.

Surprise your family with just ACTIONS. When we talk and don't do, we set those expectations too high for ourselves, knowing we might not be able to deliver. And when that doesn't happen, we get even more down on ourselves. So, just do it!

It's okay to have someone hold you accountable

There are seasons where I travel a lot for ministry. It wasn't always this way, but one season it seemed I was in a different state every other month. And most of the time, I am by myself, and Sasha knows where I am at every second, every minute.

It's not that she doesn't trust me, it's holding me accountable. It has been like this since day one that we got back together. She knows all my passcodes and she is welcome to look at my phone anytime. I don't hide or keep things from her.

Even to this day, I let her know when I am leaving the gym or going to lunch or to another meeting. You see, back then I would have the attitude of "I am a grown man, I don't need someone to keep tabs on me." Wrong attitude! That's why I got into so much trouble in the beginning. Waking up every morning with a clear mind and conscience is better than waking up with a regretful one.

Do you want to regain that trust back, especially with your loved ones? Let them hold you accountable! You might ask, what if you're not married or with someone? Then find someone that can hold you accountable anyway, it won't hurt. It will just make you better. Don't look at it like someone is babysitting you, look at it as a gym partner. They are helping you get stronger, and giving you that extra push you desperately need.

We have to show our family we are different. If your kids are older, tell them you love them DAILY! Even if they are mad at you, or you haven't seen them in a while. Show them you love them. Send a text, write a letter, tell them over the phone. If they are small, just be there and available to them as much as possible.

These are some KEY points that helped me regain the trust of my family. I will testify that trust is hard to gain once it's lost. However, this time, you're not gaining their trust back based on lies. Your gaining it back on good character and integrity and by doing instead of saying. And once you get that back, it's yours unless you show them otherwise.

Anytime I am away, my wife can trust me and I can trust her too. This trust was not built overnight, it was built on healing. It was built not on saying, but it was built on doing and showing. It was built with a different outlook and attitude. I am not ashamed to say my wife holds me accountable in my recovery. She is my best friend, I really don't have anyone else. She sees me at my worst, she sees me at my lowest. When I would tell her I couldn't go on anymore, she would speak life into me, she spoke hard truth! When someone doesn't want to be held accountable, it means they have something to hide, or they have too much pride and ego. I was done with all that macho attitude. I wanted a right one, with a right spirit.

I know you're probably hurting right now because you're wondering if you can ever gain that trust again — believe me, you can. But you have to understand that it's going to take some time! Nevertheless, keep at it, keep building, and KEEP DOING! All I ever wanted to do was to regain the trust of my family. I would work on other things I needed to do later. But my family needed to know that I was for real, they needed to know I was not just going to jump ship and leave them again. I wanted to put them FIRST. I was really trying, I was really doing with my actions. And I think over time, I proved that to them. Then, as months went by, that trust began to form, relationships began to build, and things improved for the better. If I can do it, so can you!

Much Love,
Anthony Torres

"Wherever you land, no matter

how misunderstood you are.

LIVE, LOVE, and

THRIVE!"

LETTER 39

THOUGHTS ON
'I DON'T WANT TO GO, BUT I AM TIRED'

I don't want to go but I'm tired
Do I really have a purpose? Or am I just blowing off to some place?
I don't want to go but I'm tired
Look at my face, it tells its own footrace
I don't want to go but I'm tired
I don't want to say goodbye, so I pray and look to the sky
I don't want to go but I'm tired
Depression, anxiety, sleepless nights, heavy heart, full mind
Will my spirit ever unwind?
I don't want to go but I'm tired
The road is long, and my feet sometimes are not strong
I don't want to go but I'm tired
Social media is our new journal, with our verbal
To shame others, to bully others, to belittle others.
Great job! You just killed someone's spirit
I don't want to go but I'm tired,
no love nor respect for humanity, we are SELFISH
and hurt others in our vanity
I don't want to go but I'm tired

Letters To My People

Republican vs. Democrat, who is right? Or better?
Will hate fix a nation? While the world's in depression
I don't want to go but I'm tired
Christian vs Christian, Church vs Church
While you draw your sword and swing it in the name of
the Lord
You pierce what beats, when all it wants is peace
I don't want to go but I'm tired
You give, you love, you help. Is it ever good enough?
You feel empty when you're snuffed
I don't want to go but I'm tired
I fight the world, I fight with people, I fight my own self
Daily I fight in HIS light
I don't want to go but I'm tired
Please don't get mad if I breakdown, and speak of death,
sometimes I just don't want this breath

I don't want to go but I'm tired
Racial tension is HIGHER than it's ever been,
When will LOVE win?
I don't want to go but I'm Tired
And so are you. But you're needed, you have PURPOSE
even if you're blowing in the wind.
Wherever you land, no matter how misunderstood you
are. LIVE, LOVE, and THRIVE!

Much love,
Anthony Torres

"When we don't take responsibility for our actions or words, we play victim"

LETTER 40

THOUGHTS ABOUT
'VICTIM MENTALITY'

I don't know why I feel the need to write this thought, but maybe it is what someone needs to hear. I am going to start off with this strong statement, but there is a lot of truth to it.

When we don't take responsibility for our actions or words, we play victim.

And not taking responsibility and playing victim will not allow our recovery to begin. Because we are always going to find someone to blame for where we are at in life. Blaming someone or something is the easy part, seeing things for what they really are can be the hard part. But having the mindset of, "You know what, I got myself here and I am okay with that" speaks volumes of your heart in recovery. It's taking the first step in embracing responsibility.

I think what I learned in my recovery when I embraced responsibility is that I was going to do whatever I can to get out of this mess that I was in. I was going to claw, scratch, and fight for every single day that I was allowed to live and have. If I messed up, I kept going. I had spent my whole life giving up when things got tough for me and I didn't want to be that guy anymore by quitting.

I got to a point and time in my life where I got tired of letting my depression get the best of me, I got tired of feeling unmotivated, tired of my past having me all balled up inside emotionally. Sometimes we just don't get tired of our same life in recovery, we really get tired of our own excuses. I needed to take charge! I needed to stop making excuses and take my life back. And, my friend, this is exactly what you need to do also.

Could I have played victim? Of course, I could. We all can! But something POWERFUL happens when we say "I messed up" or "I did this." Something happens inside when we say "This step that I am about to take, it's with no pointing fingers. It's with no passing blame on anyone or anything."

That step you're about to take comes with a lot of responsibility, a lot of moving and doing on our apart. And I truly believe that you can do it. You can also dig your way out of that hole you got yourself into! You get to decide how long you stay in that pit of playing VICTIM. The fact is, your recovery will be that much harder if you keep playing victim, and making it seem like it's everyone else's fault and not yours.

Why do we do this?

I think it's because it makes it easy for us not to accept change. We don't have to peel back the layers of why we are in this mess. We do it because we don't want to face the reality of our lives or maybe we are scared to open old wounds we have forgotten about. It doesn't allow us to see what we need to work on and do to change in our lives, to get on this road of recovery.

To be honest, even when I found my newfound faith in Christ, I was still playing victim. I was still angry. I was still trying to pass the blame on someone or some event that happened in my life. I still had a lot of issues I needed to work on and address. I had a lot of emotions I was dealing with while I was clean and sober. Then when I relapsed, I was looking for someone or something to blame, so that way I could say, "See, my life is this way because..." or "I keep going back to my old ways because...."

Eventually, I started learning more about myself and who I was and what I had become in my addiction. Once I took that step of taking responsibility for my actions and words, the healing and recovery began for me.

One thing I will say is some people play this role and don't even know it. So how can you know? Ask yourself the following questions.

Do you feel negative when you relapse?

Do you criticize everyone for not helping you?

Do you feel bitter and complain at all times?

Do you talk bad about people behind their back, because you thought they would help you when you needed them?

Do you find it difficult to see good in any situation and it's always everyone else's fault?

These could be some signs that you're playing victim and you may not even know it. I see it all the time.

Some parents were mad at me because their son or daughter got back in prison or jail, and now it's my fault because they feel I didn't help them enough, or sit down enough and talk with them more? I tell all those that I give counsel to that I am not God. I am a man. I am going to give you what I know, what I learned and what worked for me. The rest is up to you. You have to put 100 percent effort into this if you want to see change.

Some follow through and some don't.

My prayer for you is that after you have read this thought, some things will begin to stir in your heart and reflect so you can know if you are playing victim or not. This thought is short because the point is not to sit here and try to beat you up with the victim mentality.

It's trying to help you shed some light on this topic, to help you get moving in your recovery. We can always say life is not fair, courts are not fair, people are not fair, the system is broken. There is not enough help. Or maybe if I grew up this way, or if I was a different race, it would be easier. Or if had money, I can get more help. Never sit there and think of the "what ifs" or "if I had this or that." We need to start thinking about possibilities. We need to start taking responsibility and seeing a way out!

Think about this and say this to yourself, "Today is the day I take FULL responsibility for my actions, for my words and for my past. I am alive today to get myself out of this mess, to get my life in order. To fight another day to be clean and sober. I will not let these demons get the best of me.

My past won't win, my mind won't defeat me. My heart won't deceive me. I can do this! It may look dark and uncertain. There may be some pain and bruises along the way. But I am always reminded in the morning that it doesn't stay dark forever and that pain will eventually heal and those bruises of life will tell a story. Your story of how you overcame this addiction!"

Hey! I hope you enjoyed reading this, and I pray it blesses you. Get moving!

Much love,
Anthony Torres

"Our addictions sometimes wait at

our door, waiting for us to fall, to

become weak, to tempt us again

when life gets hard. This is why

we have to stay sharp and alert

in our recovery"

LETTER 41

THOUGHTS ABOUT
'RELATIONSHIP VS YOUR RECOVERY'

N ow I think this is a thought that needs to be read with an open heart and clear mind. Have you ever heard the saying "Dating someone clouds the mind."? My mom used to tell me, "Anthony, you need to stay focused on school and football. Keep your mind CLEAR and FOCUSED. Stay away from the girls!"

Hey, I get it! We all have been there before. Do you remember when we were in high school and we had a break-up with whoever we were dating and we couldn't think, or we couldn't function without them (or at least we thought)? We didn't feel like going to work, we didn't feel like doing anything. We were just down in our spirits. The break-up blues are real, I think we all can agree that relationships can cloud the mind.

I have seen this scenario play out so many times and it goes like this: A man or woman gets out of Rehab or jail or starts to clean up their life, they start coming to church, coming to programs to stay sober and clean. They start serving in the church. I see them every Sunday, and every time I see them, I hear "Pastor, call me if you need anything." Some of them are the most faithful people I know. And they will be there if we need anything.

Then, in time, God blesses them. He starts moving into their lives. God is answering their prayers. They get a job, they start making money. They get their own place to live, they go from riding a bike or getting rides everywhere to now having their own car. Their lives are being restored slowly and it's a beautiful thing to see and experience. Seeing people come from nothing and see the process of a life once in ruin be put back together will always make my heart happy.

Then after some time, I see them walk in with a new friend. Later I hear them say "Pastor, pray for us, we are dating." Now let me just say this before I go on. I am always happy to see all this start to happen in people's lives. I mean, this is what it is all about. We go from having nothing, we go from the pits of darkness and hell to the light and to the blessings God has for us. This is a good thing. And by no means am I being judgmental or critical about this topic. But I will say this, I patiently see how things eventually play out

After a short period of time, I don't see them in church anymore. They no longer come to group anymore. I hear they are missing work. A duty they once served in the church is now vacant. Of course, I text them and check on them and they respond by saying "I'm good, just been busy working." Then after some weeks, I get that phone call or text.

"Pray for me! I relapsed." Or their partner calls me and says, "He/she is back in jail."

What happened? Is the relationship they got into to blame? Well, we can't say that, we just finished talking about taking responsibility in one of the thoughts I shared. I can share what happened with you. Are you ready?

They lost focus! They lost focus on what was important in their life. They lost sight of how far they have come in recovery. They **STOPPED** doing things that were working for them in their recovery. Now we all have been there before, but the important thing is getting back on track.

Don't become idle! Sure, having a relationship is great. I mean no one wants to live a lonely life. Having a job and getting back on your feet and seeing the blessings of God that follow you is exciting! But you can't put your recovery on the back burner.

Listen, it's now 11 years that I have been clean and sober and I still have to work on things to keep me where I am. I just don't say, "I pastor a church so I have arrived," or "God is using me, I am good. I don't need to work on my recovery anymore."

NEVER! I continue to put in hard work every day. Friends, we can't afford to take days off. Not when it comes to our recovery.

I was alone for four months without anyone. I had to learn to keep working on myself every day, and if someone was going to be a part of my life, they needed to know my recovery came first. When Sasha and I got back together, I remember telling her that I found God, and I love church. I love to read my Bible. I love to watch my church shows. I didn't want this newfound faith to stop in my life, and if she could go to church, I would love it.

However, I remember telling myself I was not going to force anything on her, and I made up my mind that I was going to church, with or without her. I was going to continue to build and grow in my newfound faith with or without her.

I am happy to say that today we decided to do it together. But listen to me when I say this, your recovery needs to come first before ANY relationship. I know falling in love is great and all, but you need to fall in love with your recovery first. And whoever you date or marry needs to support you in your recovery. Your meetings, your counseling sessions, your faith, your church - whatever it is for you, you need to keep going and never stop.

I know what you're saying as you read this, "I am stronger than that. I have what I need to stay this course of being clean and sober." And that's a good thought. But I have counseled many people that were clean and sober for years, and one day, they stopped working on what they have been doing for years and went right back to their addiction. Back at shooting up, back at the bars.

Our addictions sometimes wait at our door, waiting for us to fall, to become weak, to tempt us again when life gets hard. This is why we have to stay sharp and alert in our recovery. I told someone this the other day, we can't afford to let our guard down. We need to keep growing in our faith and our recovery. When we allow other things to overshadow our recovery, this is what happens. We start to lose focus. It's easy to lose it. But we can get it back again.

Listen, don't go running to break up with your boyfriend or girlfriend, this is not what I am saying you need to do. You just need to get your priorities in order and stay with them. Have that honest conversation with your spouse if you're in a relationship. Let them understand that you need to put your recovery first, and not leave it on the back burner.

And if you're not seeing someone or not married, I just laid out some pitfalls that you can avoid.

The other thing I want to talk about is:

If you and your partner are seeking treatment apart, then you get out of rehab before them and start doing good and getting your life in order. Then one day your partner gets out and goes right back to their old life. Why are you going back to them?

I have seen this played out a million times as well and it's always the same conversation. "I am so strong in my life right now than I ever been. I have the tools to help them. THEY NEED ME."

"What if I am the key to helping them?" I said this in the early thoughts. But the fact is, you can't save them! I am going to tell you what is going to happen. They are going to eventually drag you down with them emotionally. And before you know it, you both are using and drinking again.

Love has power, but addiction is more POWERFUL!

I remember there was a girl that I really liked to be around early in my recovery. I was going to church and getting better. But she used drugs and was a drinker. I would invite her to church and she would come sometimes. I felt like I could be of help to her, and it felt good when she would say "I want a better life." But one day I gave in, and I used with her. One cocaine line turned into many. Next thing you know, I was on a 2-day binge, and it was the worst feeling ever. Lord knows I have been in this place many times, but this time, it felt different. I had come so far, to now seeing myself fail again. I left her house in the early morning and there I was again walking the streets because I had nowhere to go.

At 6am, I found the sun coming up on my face and the cold coming out of my mouth and I said, "Here I am again." later that week, I had to break up that relationship and start to re-focus on my recovery again. I don't care how many times you fall, friend, get back up!

How many times have we said that "Here I am again"? I know I said it many times. I am speaking to you today not trying to judge your life or to be negative, I am speaking because I have fallen flat on my face so many times. I spent enough time going in circles in my own emotions of my own setbacks, many days of the storms rolling in and the rain drops hitting my face, wondering if I really can get sober and clean. Having thoughts like, "Will my life be boring? How will things be?"

I am trying to help you see what can happen if we are not careful and if we put relationships first before our recovery. If your partner really loves you, really cares for you, they will support you in whatever you need to do to get where you need to be.

One thing I was thankful for was when I quit drinking, Sasha quit with me. I didn't tell her to, but she felt it in her heart. She didn't want to tempt me or be a stumbling block for me. That's been 11 years ago now and counting. And I give God all the glory for this.

I close with this, getting our lives in order after addiction is a wonderful thing. I love to hear stories of people who haven't talked to their kids or grandkids in years due to their addiction or them being locked up, and now they have a relationship with them. I love to hear stories of relationships mending back together after months of separation. I love to see that a person gets a second chance in life.

But it hurts me when I see them work so hard, put in work every single day in their recovery. then one day, they are back to their old ways, old thoughts, old addictions. And I saw it happening before they did. I told them it would happen. But they didn't listen to me. But they know I love them. I am not here to judge them or make them feel low. I am here to help them and coach them back to get going in recovery again.

I am praying for you today, friend. Keep going, remember your recovery must come first.

Much love,
Anthony Torres

"Living in the past won't let you live

or enjoy the now"

LETTER 42

THOUGHTS ABOUT
'LIVE IN THE NOW'

Let's be honest right now, you are flooded with all kinds of emotions, and you have all kinds of thoughts racing in your mind as you read this book. That was the point and the intention of my heart, that it would really make you start thinking and do some real soul searching in your life. I know some of these letters with my thoughts have been hard for you to read. Trust me, there were many late nights I shed tears on my keyboard as I wrote these words. Pain is real, and everyone in the world just wants to know if they can actually make it

And I am proud of you for picking up this book with the willingness to want a life of being sober and clean. If you were like me, I think a lot about the past and the future. And what I learned is that if we are not careful, we will miss living in the NOW. I'm sure we think about the past because of things like health issues, parole, charges against us, broken relationships, homelessness, and the pain and hurt we have gone through.

If I haven't said this before, I want to say it right now.

Your past will keep you stuck at a door, jiggling your keys trying to open it, when the door has been shut and locked.

Your key won't open it anymore. It's not yours any more to OPEN! How much time have you wasted at that door? Why are you going back to something that has already been shut and locked? Do me a favor, go to the door and break your key in the hole! You see, you have walked through that door already. You came out and went back in. Well, who locked it?

GOD! Your past has been forgiven. Why go through a door he already shut and forgave you for what happened behind that door? Every word, every hurt you caused others, every time you made a mess of your life, time that you even tried to hurt yourself. Those scars on your arms from cutting yourself are a reminder that the door is shut. They aren't bleeding anymore. Listen to me when I say that you are forgiven. Stop writing your past back on an eraser board, when it has already been erased. Look, the smudges are still there. THE DOOR IS SHUT!

We would be surprised how many people relive their past, they play the scenes over and over again in their mind. Thinking of what they could have done differently or if they should have done this or that, or said this or shouldn't have said this.

We can think about the past all we want, but I really believe that it robs us of the NOW. Hear me when I say, *"Living in the past won't let you live or enjoy the now."*

Did I rehash the past?

Of course, I did!

I thought a lot about "What if I had gotten help sooner? What would my life look like? What if I never started my business? What if Sasha and I got married when we were going to, would we be divorced now? Would we have gotten back together? What if I had gone to the military like I wanted, what would my life be today?"

I stayed at the door trying to jiggle that key. And the more I stayed there, the more depressed I got. The more heavy I became. The more living in the now became something like someone stretching my mind. I had pressure. And it all was

278

coming from my past. It all came just with me staying stuck at that door.

But when I started to understand what was happening, I had to wake up with a different focus and a new mindset and try not to go back to the place that I had come out of in my mind, and in my life. Sadly, no matter how much we rehash the past, we can't change it. It's done! The door is closed, so throw away the keys. They don't work in that keyhole anymore.

Drugs had not just robbed me of my life, they were trying to now rob me of my mind and trying to rob me of living in the now. Go throw that key from the past away and get moving. There are NEW doors with great promises for you to walk through.

The other thing I want to talk about is, looking forward to the future. I am not saying you shouldn't make plans for yourself, it's important. But try not to see too ahead that you can't live in the now. If we are not careful, we can try to make things happen to try to get ahead faster in life. I get it! We feel we wasted 10 to 20 years of our life, we can't get back, and we try to hurry the future up just a little bit. But don't rush things!

What if I told you it could take up to 5 years, maybe 8, to be where you fully need to be. I was 32 and I was 5 years into my recovery, I was still picking up the pieces to my past. Now, even at 11 years into it, I feel I have come a long way but trust me when I say I am still seeing those pieces being put back together in my life.

Don't rush things, don't marry the first person that says hello because it's been months of loneliness. Don't go try to juggle too much to get ahead faster, pace yourself and soon you will see things start to come into place.

In 2009, as a family, we lived with my in-laws for almost a year before we moved out. It took me 3 jobs to feel secured financially to get my family our own house again. And to top it off, I was out of work for almost 6 months after I started to clean up my life. We drove a small car around for almost 2 years, and we are a family of 5.

Sometimes when my oldest daughter would visit, I would have to take two trips to church to drop everyone off. We lived in a 2 bedroom 1 bath town home. Caleb, my son, shared a room with Sasha and I for some time, and the girls shared a room together, before we were able to get another home.

Our first Christmas as a family in 2009 was very tough, we had no money for presents or even to get a Christmas tree. This was hard for me as a father because I always had a good job to provide for my kids and we always had what we needed. But this Christmas would be different, I couldn't work up the strength to tell the kids we have no money for presents, or could we afford a tree. That was a time we truly got a glimpse of what Christmas was about. It's not about gifts or money, it's about Family and Christ. When you have that, sometimes that's all you need around the holidays.

Sadly, Sasha's mom had to lend us a tree from her classroom where she taught 1st grade, just so we could have a Christmas tree in our home.

Can you imagine how I felt as a father? If it wasn't for my in-laws, we probably wouldn't have had a Thanksgiving either. I am here to tell you, when addictions plagued my family and tore us apart, it was a time we really needed to come together as a family and we did, in the beginning and even today. We are all we have, and all we will ever need.

I can say that as a father, I wore my shoes till they formed holes in them to make sure my kids had what they needed. I remember one time Sasha was telling me to get new shoes because they were falling apart. Those shoes probably did have holes in them and were falling apart, but inside my heart, for once in our lives, my family wasn't.

We enjoyed shopping at thrift stores for clothes and shoes, because we had little money. We had to start all over again, from the ground up. Everything we have today, is because we have worked really hard believing that we all deserved a great life. I know the struggles really well. And I don't forget where I have come from nor how far I have come.

When it was all said and done in starting to pick up the pieces of our lives left by addiction, it wasn't till a few years ago that we felt we were in a place we needed to be - with our home, our cars and where we finally felt okay financially. It took us nine years! That's right, nine years to be where we needed to be.

This is why it's so important that you live in the now. Focus on the now. Be strengthened in the now. Believe in the now. Do what you need to do in your recovery in the now. Sit back, be patient and just watch things start to shape and form for your future.

Now, I turn 40 in seven days, and I am working on things for the future. But I have learned not to rush things. Living in the now is where I want to be. When I am 45 or 50, God willing, I would see things flourish that I have set in motion when I was seven days shy of my 40th birthday.

Remember, get out of the past and don't rush the future. You need to live in the now in your recovery. Don't get discouraged when things are not working fast enough for you. Sometimes starting from the ground up is the best way for us to start, because we can do things right in our lives for once. We have seen the mistakes we have made and we can learn from them. Keep going!

Much love,
Anthony Torres

"Your surroundings, your friends,

your environment, your habits, your

thinking, your heart, your

relationships, and maybe even your

job. Must change in your

recovery!"

LETTER 43

THOUGHTS ABOUT
'EMBRACE CHANGE'

I t seemed like the weekend was more like the devil's playground for me. I drank and used during the week, and even when I got sick in the morning, I would throw up, pop Advil and drink a V-8 drink and I was ready for my work day.

But the weekend? It felt like I invited more of my demons to play with me on my playground. It was like we locked hands and enjoyed each other's company. I enjoyed them whispering in my ear, feeling the hot air coming from their lips, making promises to me. I think most of the time I didn't drink to have fun anymore. I drank not to feel anymore. It seemed I didn't do drugs to get high anymore. But to kill my spirit, to kill my hurt of being nothing, my pain of no purpose. To kill what I had become. To kill me!

I turned into a street cluck and I hated it. I hated sitting down there looking over this brick wall we used to have at our old home, I would see the sun come up from Organ mountains. It was 7am and I was still drunk, waiting for my drug dealer to wake up just so I can continue to kill my spirit. The sad part was he lived across the street from me, and I would walk over there when I knew he was up. I'm sure his wife was not happy with me.

I had my routine in my addiction and it went on for years like that. Everyone knew that on Fridays, I was at happy hour somewhere in a bar. I was being hell on wheels, like my mother would say. I was a reflection of my own heart and it was dark and I didn't care who I hurt or what I did. I look back now and wonder how I survived my devil's playground. I was there for too long, almost 9 long years of hell. Dark and lonely!

Now today, I am in bed by 9:30pm and that's seven days a week. Things are really different now. Now my days consist of watching movies with my son and wife. It's now "A funny movie" or "Action movie" vs. "Cocaine" or "Meth." Decisions of "do I stay up late to finish the movie" vs" do I smoke it or snort it." Now it's popcorn and pickles vs. shots and Corona. I don't spend my nights or mornings throwing up anymore, it's now Starbucks or McDonald's coffee. I don't spend my nights holding a gun to my head anymore, now I hug and embrace my children and have wonderful conversations about life. I don't spend dark weeks in my depression anymore, I spend my weeks trying to be a better father and husband.

They say time flies when you're having fun, I say it flies when you have a sober and clean life and are doing the right things for once. Sometimes in our addiction, time just dragged, and those drugs took us with it.

A lot has changed in the past 11 years, me and my wife talk about it all the time. It was like a bad dream, a nightmare, something that we lived and experienced. But it's still hard to embrace all that we have been through and where we are at today. Embracing change is something you have to do. I have said this many times, in recovery, you don't just change some things about your life, you have to change EVERYTHING.

Your surroundings, your friends, your environment, your habits, your thinking, your heart, your relationships, and maybe even your job. You have to put yourself in a position to win, not to go backward. Most of the time, we go back because nothing in our lives has changed. The only thing that has changed is that we made up our minds to get better. But it's still the same environment, same friends, same habits, same thinking. And when that happens, it's more likely we go back to using.

Change is something you're going to have to embrace, don't look at your life as getting boring. Look at your life as being changed and getting better. So you can stop drinking, stop doing drugs, stop making a mess out of your life and letting your loved ones down.

I think embracing change is hard because we have done some things for so long. We feel like we are doing something wrong. Like we don't deserve a good life. We have spent half of our lives making a mess out of our lives for so long. We are afraid of doing good.

Listen to me! Embrace your new life and don't be afraid of it. You have embraced wrong for so long, it's time to embrace good. Time to embrace change. It's time to Embrace your kids, your family, your wife, your husband, your new job, your new goal.

They say most of the time that when people get out of prison, it's so hard for them to adjust to being out on the streets. Think about doing the same routine for 5-20 years, then one day you're out of prison, doing something different. Most of the time, some people go back to prison because sometimes it's all they know, it can be hard for them to adjust. If you're reading this and you're getting out soon to go home to your family, I am praying that you can adjust and enjoy this great life that God has given you. Don't be afraid to try something new!

You may not be in prison, but that prison of addiction is not in you anymore. It doesn't have to have a grip on you anymore. It doesn't have to keep you hostage anymore. It's okay to embrace your life in recovery. It's okay to embrace healthy thoughts and healthy patterns.

Change is something we don't adjust to well as people, even if it's good, because we are creatures of habit. This is why you create a healthy one for yourself. Do me a favor before we end this letter.

Tell yourself right now, "It's okay to embrace this Change!"

It's a good thing!
It's a new thing!
It's a new YOU!

It's something that has to happen! Your change is not meant to harm or hurt you. It's meant to help you. Embrace it, love it and live it, friend. I write this with a smile on my face because I know what you're feeling. You're saying "I am not used to this."

Hey! Life is better when you're not looking over your shoulders anymore. Life is better when you're not waking up with hangovers anymore. Life is great when you can look your kids in the eyes with no more regrets. Life is great when you know your spouse is not going to leave you because you didn't come home last night from a binge and drunk night.

Life is rewarding when you can open your eyes in the morning and once your feet hit the floor, you can be at peace in your heart because you know those demons won't chase you anymore.

You don't have to run, those days are over. I remember I got tired of running, so I embraced those demons. Not anymore. Put the Nike's away and enjoy your van slippers. Enjoy your NEW life. Your running days are over, friend!

Embrace the good change, friends. Good things are coming, blessings are following you. You're going to make it. And you're going to be okay!

I want to end with this, I don't want to go back to my old life and I know you don't want to either. So don't let go of this change. I want you to embrace it and never let go. Do what you need to do to stay in it.

Much love,
Anthony Torres

"Dear momma, where would I be

without your love and prayers"

LETTER 44

'DEAR MOMMA'

Dear momma, I wonder what you must have felt emotionally knowing you were going to have a baby at 16. Your whole high school, derailed by teen pregnancy. I'm not even sure you made your senior prom because of me. I have seen pictures of you being a cheerleader. I hope you were able to at least finish some of the dreams you have set before yourself.

When the reality of being a mother hit you, instead of picking a College degree, you spent your time picking up an infant. Instead of changing classes you didn't like for College, you spent time changing my diaper. Your Sacrifice for me, momma, never goes unnoticed.

The day I was born, I'm sure you looked into my brown eyes and wondered what kind of kid I would turn into, what kind of man I would grow up to be. But I'm sure you never thought you would have to deal with a son that was lost in addiction to drugs and alcohol. A son full of anger. A son full of pride. A son dealing with depression and wanting to end his life. A son screaming at the God that created him. A son who struggled so much, yet stayed silent. I stayed silent for so long that nobody knew that I was eating away in my insides, like maggots on raw meat. A son full of promise, yet would fall short due to addictions.

Dear momma, I bet you didn't see that in my little brown eyes as you held me in my little blanket in 1981. And everything that happened was not your fault, sometimes life is just life, momma, you know that. I have so much memories of you being brave, fighting wars that were never meant for you to fight, you fought them bravely. I remember you being such a good mother, making sure me and my brother had everything we needed. I would see you come straight from work, right into the kitchen. We never went without anything! And you made sure of that. You always put yourself last, mom. And I saw this modeled for me daily.

Dear momma, I still remember many nights hearing you cry. I'm sure you were wondering what your life would now be because of your divorce. I know it was hard on you, dealing with this after the death of your parents. I can only imagine what was going through your mind knowing you had to start all over again, knowing how alone you felt, how empty you felt. Grieving every day!

Feeling like you had no voice. I hope my smile and my brother's face brought you joy in the morning. I hope we were enough for you to keep going, momma. Enough for you to keep fighting another day. And I feel guilty saying this, because I was so upset at you. I remember blaming you for how things ended up and I am not even sure why. Forgive me! All I know is that I was in a different state. And I missed my father. Why couldn't I wake up with both of you in the house? I also hope that the divorce was not because of me and my brother.

Dear momma, I got in so much trouble. I hung around so many people that were such a bad influence on me. That night I got jumped and stabbed, I thought you were going to be so mad at me. Yet, you loved me and took care of me. I had promised to stay out of trouble, at least I did for a little while.

Dear momma, you finally got your Bachelor's degree. I was so proud of you. You have always taught me to reach for my dreams, even if they were out of my reach.

Dear momma, I am sorry you got sick. I remember hearing the doctor say, "If you had come in a day late, you would have died." I was so angry at God that day, I cursed him. I told him this is why I didn't believe in him, he was a mean and ugly God. I didn't pray, but I did go out and get drunk. I rode around on my motorcycle from bar to bar, city to city. I did so much drugs that night I don't even remember how I got home. Leukemia would get the best of your body, but not the best of your spirit. Even to this day, you're still fighting for every year it took from you. I love you, momma.

Dear momma, I know in the end, you had to show me tough love during that season of my addictions. The doors were shut, but your hearts were open. Your minds were troubled, but I was in God's hands, as you would say. I know you and my step dad didn't know what to do with me. My denial kept me longer in that season than it should have been. Yet, your patience was growing thin.

Dear momma, I love you so much! I think if I had lost you a long time ago, I am not sure what my life would have been. I had already been drinking so much, it would have sent me over the edge. You earned your name "Hood momma" because momma didn't play. You were tough, stern, and hard on us. Yet you were caring, loving, and always made sure we had what we needed. You loved me in my addictions. And you did what any mother would do for their child, which was to PRAY.

I remember you saying, "I am just waiting to get that phone call that you died." I can only imagine what your nights were like when I would show up drunk on my motorcycle. I just showed up to give you a kiss before I went out to get lost and danced with the devil. Because there were many nights I was not sure If I was going to make it.

Dear momma, when you dropped me off at Rehab. You kissed me on my cheek as my hands were shaking and you hugged me, with tears in your eyes. You said, "I love you, son, you will get through this." And I am sure it felt like the day you sent me off to school. You were scared but glad I was going.

Dear momma, I'm doing it! I'm getting my life in order, thanks to God. The day I started to clean up my life, you said "I can now die in peace. You're going to be okay and I don't have to worry about getting a phone call that you died anymore." I am sorry, momma, that I put you through that. I hope and pray that I make you proud now.

Dear momma, where would I be without your love and prayers. I know we are not as close as we need to be, but you are still a part of my heart and part of my recovery, and for that, I am thankful. I love you, momma. Be at peace, I am going to be okay.

Much love,
Your son

"I was the criminal on the cross.

LORD, REMEMBER ME!"

LETTER 45

THOUGHTS ABOUT
'OVERDOSING'

As long as I have the privilege and honor to interact with addicts on a weekly basis, my heart will continue to shatter every time I hear these words, "He/she died of an overdose this morning." One thing I often say after hearing this is "That could have been me" or "God why didn't I die in my addictions?" Then I spend my day grieving for the family, as I take it very hard. I always tell my class, "You want to break a pastor's heart? Let him get that phone call you passed due to an overdose."

I look back and think *Why not me?* I gave my body every opportunity to shut down and die, yet I am still here. Was this part of my purpose to survive? Was it part of God's plan to use me? I think so, yet, yearly, I bury sons, daughters, mothers, and fathers due to addictions. I hear countless mothers say "He was a good kid, he just couldn't shake these drugs" or a father saying "She loved her kids so much and planned to go to school, yet she just couldn't let go of the one thing that was destroying her life, drugs." Or the wife that says "He loved the beer bottle more than me and it killed him, his liver shut down."

It's like when my heart begins to heal, it will shatter again with news like this. I feel my depression begin to poke my side, not with one finger but two. I feel anxiety begin to plague my mind. I toss and turn at night because I can hear the screams of a mother. I can hear their sobbing cries of "Why!" I see their loved one's lifeless body lying on the floor, or hooked up to a ventilator machine and I see all the pain that they have dealt with. Because their cold-lifeless face tells a story to me, your bruised veins that you once jabbed with a needle loaded with heroin tells your pain. As I see these images, I then battle in my own heart, to heal again, as I process these things I have seen. I distant myself from my family, as I am in my own world, and it's that constant war within me. Sometimes I still wonder why God brought back my family if days were going to be like this.

Overdosing will happen, to the poor, the rich, the saved and un-saved, the righteous and unrighteous. But I always had this one question, "Since I found Christ, and I gave my heart to him, knowing that I was still struggling in my addiction, if I Overdosed, would God had sent me to hell?" I thought about that a lot.

I am about to share something I found out with you, that religious and legalist people will have a field day with my statement and ridicule me for it and maybe even call me a false prophet. Here is my conclusion to my questions: No, he wouldn't have sent me to hell. Here is why; it's my Belief in Him and His Love for me!

You see, I spent my whole life not believing. I spent my whole life searching for something. In 2009 Christ found me, in my mess and in my addiction. For once in my life, I put my trust and BELIEF in him. Something I never did before.

In Luke 23, there is a story of two criminals on the cross with Jesus (keep in mind they all were going to eventually die). One criminal was heaping insults at Jesus, mocking him (I was that guy mocking years ago). The other one was telling the criminal to be quiet, basically sticking up for Jesus. Then he said something that I still can never get out of my spirit. He looked at Jesus vs42 and said "Jesus, remember me when you come into your Kingdom." (This was me in 2009)

I didn't want an INVITE, I just wanted to be remembered.

What Jesus said next speaks volumes. If you read the story, Jesus NEVER EVER SAID "What church did you belong to? How much money did you give to the church? What denomination did you claim (sounds hoodish, don't it?) Did you get baptized? (which I think it's important to do if we can)" He didn't say "How good were you?"

He said in vs43 "I ASSURE you (with confidence, no doubts) TODAY you will be with me in paradise (Heaven).

It's not what the man said, it's what he BELIEVED IN. WHO HE BELIEVED IN. And that was Jesus. He never doubted Jesus on the cross even though the other man did. He just believed. Talk about mind blowing. You see, we love to judge someone on the outside (criminal on the cross). God looks at the inside (heart of belief). I say it all the time, we will be shocked who is in heaven!

The other one is HIS love for me!

My whole life I knew the love of my parents. But I NEVER felt the love of my creator like I did in 2009. My whole life I was taught that if something bad was happening to me, it was because God was mad at me. Well, I must have been a really bad person, because it seemed nothing ever went right in my life. This is no healthy way of growing up feeling like this.

One night, as I read the Bible (I had no idea what I was reading, I just read), I had that thought in my mind of relapsing, and what if I overdosed, would God send me to hell? Would he let me die in my demons, then send me to hell? I stumbled on this scripture that I am going to share with you. I didn't stumble on it by accident, it was meant for me to read it. To share with a world full of judgy pants! Here it goes:

Romans 8:35-38

35 Can anything ever separate us from Christ's love? Does it mean he no longer loves us if we have trouble or calamity, or are persecuted, or hungry, or destitute, or in danger, or threatened with death?

36 As the Scriptures say, "For your sake we are killed every day; we are being slaughtered like sheep."

37 No, despite all these things, overwhelming victory is ours through Christ, who loved us.

38 And I am convinced that nothing can ever separate us from God's love. Neither death nor life, neither angels nor demons, neither our fears for today nor our worries about tomorrow—not even the powers of hell can separate us from God's love.

NOR demons nor HELLS POWER!

If you know anything about addiction, it is HELL! Those demons are so strong sometimes. Why do we think it kills so many people we love? But I have come to the conclusion that "NO! God's love is more powerful than my addiction. My belief in Jesus is more powerful than my death."

It wouldn't have been how I wanted to leave, nor how I wanted my fight within me to end. But if it did happen, then I would know my fighting would be over, and my spirit was with Jesus forever.

When I relapsed, how many times did my soul within me scream "Lord, remember me! I don't want to do this anymore. I am tired. Help me, God, to kick these addictions. I was the criminal on the cross. LORD, REMEMBER ME!"

I found something that I couldn't let go of, and that was my newfound faith. I was in war every single day in my addictions, and in my recovery. But I never let my foot off the pedal, friend. I kept fighting daily. Learning more about me, and about God. And no matter how bad it got for me sometimes, I continued to believe and continued to love Him as He loves me.

Listen to me, in this hard life, and this cruel world, in your addictions, in your recovery, in your dark times, and your lowest moments, I need you to do me a favor. Never stop saying "Lord, remember me" and never stop believing that your life is worth more than what you see. Keep at it, brother and sister! Keep fighting.

Trust me when I say God knows every battle that we experience and go through. I believe in the times of hardship and dark season, He is not seeing if we can have it all together. He is still seeing if we need Him, seeing if we will still reach out to Him. I surely don't want to be like the criminal that was mocking him, even knowing that he was going to die. He didn't care about death, his heart was still darkened. I want to continue to be like the other criminal on the cross. In the season of the unknown, trusting him and believing in him for my life, no matter what that looks like.

Because according to the statistics of addiction, you and I should not be here today. But you reading this today is not by accident, and I am not just here writing just because I want to. We are here today because we got a second chance AGAIN! Don't waste it. Let's get better. Let's continue to be sober and clean. Remember, let's continue to have the words on our lips "Lord, remember me."

Much love,
Anthony Torres

"I am thankful for the weak moments that I had in my life, when every bit of my being was weak – my heart, my mind, my body and spirit. I am okay with WEAK moments, because He is not weak.

He is strong. Therefore, I am also strong!"

LETTER 46

THOUGHTS ABOUT
'2 AM'

It was a long but great day at work in 2010. After 6 months of hunting for a job, I finally landed one. I was finally getting back on my feet. That night, I laid my head on my pillow, very tired and getting ready for the next day.

For once in my life, my mind was clear. I was at peace in my heart. I may not like that I had to stay at my in-laws' or that I was starting all over again in my life. But we were all together as a family and that was important to me.

It was 2am, and I woke up in panic. While I was breathing, my right side of my chest was hurting. My heart began to race. I got up to use the restroom. I then turned on the faucet and put water on my face. I felt pain in my chest when I breathe, and I felt like a fish out of a water tank. My breath became more shallow. And I could feel my heart was about to come out of my chest.

I opened the door and told Sasha to call the ambulance, in panic she called. I sat down on the seat of the toilet and all I could do was pray. "God, watch over my family while I'm gone." I was ready at that moment to die, to meet my God. Ambulance showed up and hooked me up to an EKG machine. The words out of the paramedic were "Your heart is okay for a 29-year-old. I think what you had was a panic attack."

What?! What in the world did I have to panic about at 2am in the morning? I was asleep, a very peaceful sleep at that. I have heard about this anxiety and panic attacks. I didn't believe people who are affected by these attacks. I always thought they were faking it and seeking attention. But I can say it's real and it happens. But I began to think why now? I have never dealt with it before, just my depression from time to time, but why this anxiety attack now? What was I worried about? What was going on? Would this happen again? Unfortunately, it did.

2am seems to be a good bed time for me, or sometimes no sleep at all. Most times at night, I say, "I can't sleep" or "It's too hot" or "My mind won't shut off. What is wrong with me?" as I pull the covers off of me to get up from fighting with my sleep. I get up and walk around, read, scroll on Facebook, read again, get a glass of water and see what the night brings. Most times I just start my day.

I think ever since I have been a pastor, there have been maybe ten Sundays that I have preached with zero sleep. On Saturdays, if I find myself tossing and turning, I am at the church at 3am getting ready for the morning.

My wife now goes from "What's wrong?" to "Anything I can help with?" Sometimes my mind just won't shut off. I think too much. I feel too much - sadness, pain, death, hurt, I feel it all. I am more sensitive in my spirit and heart like never before. And I really don't know why. I wonder if it's a gift God wants me to have, so I don't lose sight of what ministry really is. I don't know. But sometimes I sit and wonder if there is something wrong with me.

I have my own mental issues in my mind. Is it the past drug use that messed me up? PTSD? Call it what you want. But I know it's there. And I can't shake it. Sometimes I feel like Paul in the Bible, pleading with God to take this thorn on my side away from me.

This is why I don't need drama, gossip, backstabbing friends, nor negativity in my life. And you don't either, friends. Your heart has to be guarded, it has to.

I know what you're thinking, but you have Jesus, right? Absolutely! And this is enough for me. Enough to keep me going, enough to get me past those nights, enough to finish this LIFE he has for me. You think life is rough? Try it sober and clean. I got Jesus, ask yourself, what do you have?

It's just a simple question for us to ask ourselves, what keeps us going when the rubber hits the road? Because when we get on the road to life, the road to recovery, it can get bumpy and hard.

Late nights seem to get the best of me, my thoughts overshadow me like a cloud mixed with hail and rain, ready to unleash its assault on me. And when it comes, I feel hopeless. Bad things come and go in and out of my mind, it's a scene in my mind that plays too many times. And it's at that time I wish I could get some relief. I can't stand myself when this happens, and I feel weak and helpless. Am I not reading God's word enough? Am I not praying enough? Am I not spiritual enough? Am I not Christian enough?"

Do you know Job in the Bible?

It's like I see the devil saying to God, "Your servant, Anthony, let me have him, let me! I can't get him at the bars anymore. I can't get him alone in the garage when he was all doped up anymore. I can't get him anymore at the desert when he had a gun to his head. I definitely can't get to him when he reads your POWERFUL word or while he is in church or tempt him in his study time. But let me have him when he gets weak and going off little sleep! Let me kick him when he is down. Let me bruise his head with my foot. Let me! Let me get to his mind. Let me mess with his emotions for a bit. And he will get tired, he will get worn out and curse you to your face. He will quit!"

I know what you're saying, "Can this really happen?" Well, according to Job, most things are father-filtered. So sometimes I just see that playing out.

During my day, I seem okay, then when I sit for a while sometimes, the assault begins. According to a counselor, my busyness is the solution for my mental breakdowns. Is she right? I don't know, I just keep my head in the Bible. I keep reading His word, and stand on His promises. He holds me together, He keeps me sane. He is my glue when I feel like falling apart.

The purpose of this thought is this: you might deal with emotions that you have never dealt with before. NEVER in my time of addictions did I deal with these kinds of emotions that I have dealt with today. They get intense sometimes, I never thought as much as I do now. I don't know if it's because of my calling of pastoring, that I see a lot or deal with a lot. I really don't know what it is. I don't want to put blame on anything or over-analyze things.

But I know I feel different emotionally now vs. back then in my addictions. Not sure if you deal with this, but just want to help in any way with this thought, to let you know there is nothing wrong with you. Drugs and alcohol numb our emotional state, but when we don't have that numbing anymore, we begin to have all kinds of emotions that we have never dealt with before.

I am trying not to turn into this guy who shuts down with his family all the time when this happens to me. I played that game in my addictions for far too long. For a while there, my wife thought she was doing something wrong, but in reality, it was me. I would just go into shutdown mode and keep to myself. Just down in my spirits for no reason, up late at night with no warning.

I lack peaceful thoughts sometimes. Am I happy? Most of the time I think I am. I am not using anymore, my family is with me and I am being used by God in a way that I couldn't imagine, even though I think I am not worthy to be used by him. But when it comes to my mind, sometimes I wonder why I think about some of the things I think about.

But I do have JOY in my heart? I love my family. And I love that I am not lost in my addictions anymore. I am putting things in place, so I can get my mind at peace. I am working on things, so I can be an overcomer. I didn't give up in my addictions, I am not giving up now.

I write this because maybe you deal with emotions that you have never dealt with before, being away from your addictions. Listen to me when I say nothing is wrong with you, I think most of us just spent our lives not feeling anything in our addiction. We had our pity parties when we needed to, but to numb everything we dealt with was good for us. Putting a pause on that emotion was something we were good at, we mastered it for so long. It's not paused or numb anymore, we are dealing with LIFE. And doing it clean and sober. Of course, that will come with new challenges, but you can do this!

Hopelessness is what I had in my last two years of my addiction. I would use more and more anytime I felt that way. I'm sure we all have felt that in our addictions. But now, we can't use anymore, we have to deal with it or get through those emotions that life brings to us. Some of us deal with PTSD, we deal with things so deep that nobody knows about. But I write this to say you're not alone in whatever you are feeling. There is a pastor in New Mexico that is warring, praying and fighting with you. Dealing with these new emotions being sober and clean can be challenging in your recovery, because you are getting out of that addictions, now finding new things coming up emotionally. But you can find healthy ways to process this when they come up.

Just understand today that you're loved! I tell my church every Sunday, trust God. Not with just the big things, but with the little things as well. I am not getting preachy on you, but there is something bigger than our emotions. And that is Jesus. I don't know where I would be without these words:

2 Corinthians 12:10 That is why, for Christ's sake, I delight in weaknesses, in insults, in hardships, in persecutions, in difficulties. For when I am weak, then I am strong.

I am thankful for the weak moments that I had in my life, when every bit of my being was weak — my heart, my mind, my body and spirit. I am okay with WEAK moments, because He is not weak. He is strong. Therefore, I am also strong!

There is nothing wrong with us, we are more normal than we have ever been, friends. Life will be life and things will always come up. We are just new souls trying to learn a new way of living. And we shall continue to live, friends.

Don't get down If you're feeling a certain way. I have talked with many people who feel there is really something wrong with them because they are feeling a certain way emotionally that they have never felt before. I truly believe:

It's just a new way of living for us, don't be discouraged. My heart and prayers are with you! Keep at it.

Much love,
Anthony Torres

"Don't think you're too far gone to

be found or too broken to be fixed,

or too damaged to be

RESTORED"

LETTER 47

Thoughts about
'Broken to Restore'

My wife has a gift, a very unique gift that I pay for out of my own pocket. It's called RESTORING furniture! I know because I buy the pieces for her, and now my garage is her storage room. We have been together for 20 years, so now I don't even argue with her about her projects. I just say, where do I pick it up and how much is it?

She will share an idea with me about a chair or a dresser she saw online. And I tell her all the time, "I don't see it, but whatever you want honey." She sees something that can be restored, and God gave her an eye for it.

For me, if I am being honest, all I see is junk and something that is old and should be thrown in the trash. Why waste all that time restoring something, when you can buy something brand new. But again, this is my opinion. But I tell you what, when she is done with her projects, I am like, "Okay! I see it now." She saw this all along in something that I never did. Think about this for a minute:

You're broken right now, people will have their strong opinions about you. Sadly, those opinions don't go away. You're in a place of addiction or in recovery and things are broken. Your job, your relationships, your money issues, you got case charges, probation, custody battles - this list is endless, and deep down inside you're like, "I can't take this no more. If I have one more bad day, I just might go back to drinking. I might go back to shooting up again. I might snort coke again. I might smoke that ice again." So you wait on your heels for that one bad day so you can go back to using again.

You're broken and the world wants to throw you away, and they just might have. People look at you like I looked at the trashy furniture that my wife wanted to restore and they say "I don't see it. I don't see what you see. I don't see something that can be restored, I see TRASH!" People say "I see someone who has made a mess out of their lives for so long. He/she can never change!"

People can be nasty and ugly with the words they say and it hurts, trust me, I know. Those people are writing you off. The world does not stop coming at you, so you can catch your breath in recovery. It doesn't and it won't. It will suffocate you and keep you from reaching your destination if you let it or you give in to the noise of what others say or think about you.

Listen to me when I say this, don't think you're too far gone to be found or too broken to be fixed, or too damaged to be RESTORED. Being Broken is not a bad thing, sometimes it's a good thing. Because our whole life, we tried to be something that we weren't. We lived a lie for a very long time.

Let God shape you and into what you were destined to do, what you were meant to become in life. Sober and clean, and on a mission to change the world, to be a good father, good mother, a great husband or wife, and to find purpose in your life.

I know you're thinking, *I have been this way for a VERY long time, not sure if there is any hope for me or any change in me.* As long as you have a heartbeat and breath in your lungs, there is always hope and possibility for change. But this will depend on how much you want to bend, how much you want to give, how much you want to let go of old attitudes, let go of learned behavior, let go of every generational curse you have been filling in your current life. You have to let go of all that so you can get to that place you need to be.

I want to give you three quick points to get you back on track.

This is something that worked for me, because the only way I know is my way. I spent 28 years trying to fix me, trying to put me back together.

Let God restore you

Piece by piece, and thought by thought. Let him invade every area of your life, every area of your heart. What have you been holding on to for so long? What needs to be healed? What do you need to let go? What do you need to forgive? What has been keeping you in a prison within yourself for so long?

This will hurt a little bit, but some things will get exposed in your life. But this is good, exposing things in your life allows you to see yourself from a different angle so you can change some things in your life.

One thing that was exposed to me was my pride and ego. I had too much of it for too long. We have to let this go. Pride keeps God out of your hearts, while ego stops him from penetrating it. How many of us have said, "I got myself in this mess, I will get myself out"? That's pride and ego talking.

Not only that, but the man I thought I was wasn't the man He wanted me to be. I had been a man of ignorance and denial. I was a man of hate and anger, the person who said "My way or the highway."

I don't think I ever learned how to properly treat a woman in my life unless I needed something from them. I had a lot of baggage when I started to clean up. I had a weak personality and got sucked into whatever I could with drugs. If it got me high, I wanted to try it. If it was a new smoke, I wanted to smoke it. If it was a new drink, you guessed it. I was going to drink it. I had a lot of learned behavior that I needed to unlearn. And learn a new way of living, a new way of thinking.

I was broken, in every way possible. To the point that I didn't know if I could ever be restored in all areas of my life. It was one BIG mess, but I sat back and watched God work. I did my part, and He really did His. God is still working in my life today. Not sure how you feel about this point, but this is a starting point for me and I think it could be for you as well. How open and honest are you willing to be?

The second point is:

Make every day COUNT

Sadly, we won't get back those years we wasted in our addiction, but we can learn from them. In your recovery, you have to do your best to make every day count. With your family, with your career, with your school, with your classes or group time. We cannot, I repeat, we cannot afford to take a day off. When we get relaxed and get idle for too long. We start to slip, we get lazy and our minds start to wander, then we go back to flirting with the darkness again. And eventually, if we are not careful, we will find ourselves relapsing. And then we find ourselves going backward instead of forward. And it won't start in one day, it starts slowly and, eventually, we will see a pattern of things that we have neglected or stopped doing. Then we find ourselves in our mess again.

This is why it's so important that you make every day count. Rest when you need to, of course, but we must keep our minds sharp, our hearts guarded and our spirit on alert. We can't have a lazy recovery.

If you're not a reader, I hope you will become one, this will help focus your mind. This is what has worked for me. I am always finding ways to learn more. Don't miss your meetings and do what you need to do to make every day count. I think those in recovery have to be some of the most self-disciplined people around. We have to be. We have seen our lives when we were not disciplined in the things we needed to do. I hope you start working toward recovery. A recovery life is a disciplined one.

My hope is that as you read this and apply it to your life, you will make every day count. Remember, put in work every single day, in whatever that looks like for you.

The last point is:

Don't get discouraged too quickly

Sometimes in my recovery, it seemed NOTHING wanted to go right. I would take three steps forward then something would happen and I would find myself five steps back. There were many times I wanted to throw in the towel. Many times I wanted to say, "This is not worth it, all this trouble and push back. I quit." My life seemed easier in my addiction (Of course, we know this is a lie), but this is what it felt like. It seemed like when I wanted to do good, life would remind me that it was in charge.

In your time of brokenness, you have to make sure you don't get discouraged too quickly. You need to tell yourself and prepare yourself that you might have some times of setbacks and this is okay. We have to go from saying "I can never catch a break" to "This setback won't break me." But don't get discouraged too quickly. WHY? Because breakthrough is coming in your life.

We all find ourselves in a time of discouragement if we are really honest, but it's what we do in that moment that is the key. That is staying in the race, staying in it no matter what happens, no matter how we feel or think. We have to make up our minds NOW that we are in this for the long haul in our recovery. To see it come to a full circle.

Anytime I have the feeling of giving up, I was reminded that when Titanic was built, it took 14,000 men to build it. And it took around three years for it to be FULLY built and completed before it sailed the sea.

How many of you know that it takes patience and seeing things come together in time? I bet you there were many workers who got discouraged and wanted to quit. But they kept working, they kept dreaming and believing. All the hard work and dedication paid off. The Titanic is probably a bad illustration in making my point because we all know what happened to the Titanic. It sunk!

But you're not going to sink, friend, you're going to strive and complete your goals. I know you can do it. I know you're capable of seeing this through. But you can't get discouraged too quickly. I have seen many women and men give up too quickly because they didn't see things happen fast enough in their life. They gave up on that breakthrough, and it was right around the corner.

You're going to come out of this stronger and better like never before. Your past was meant to break you to the point of no return, to the point of never being healed or restored. But you're going to make it! It's going to make you a better person today, for your family and for yourself.

I can't wait to see how your life plays out. Let's go!

Much love,
Anthony Torres

"Allow that heart to be searched, friend. Go deep, go wide and don't stop till every inch and area of your heart is searched and things are exposed"

LETTER 48

Thoughts about
'Alone: Part 2'

I n part 1, I talked about you being okay to be alone. In this thought, I want to share with you what being alone taught me. I mean let's be honest, no one likes to be alone; waking up alone, going shopping alone, going to the movie alone. And if you're going to church alone, sometimes that could be the worst feeling because everyone is with their family. I have been there, friend.

Living life alone in prison, rehab, or even jail can also feel like torture to us inside. No phone calls, no support, just you alone, and knowing that every step you take is done with no support system. But I was okay being alone in that time and all I could do was pray it wasn't long term for me. I mean, I had people to talk to, I had people go hang out with from time to time. But I am talking about just going through my recovery alone, relapsing and knowing I had no one to share it with. Struggling and discouraged and no one to vent to. Days that I felt good and alive and no one to share it with. But I knew this was just a season of being alone and how you view this time and what you do with it is up to you. This is what being alone taught me in my recovery.

Three quick thoughts to help you.

It was a time for me to reflect

This was a time I had to reflect on my own life and ask why I was here in this moment. Why I was far away from my kids. What I needed to do to get better. And things that I needed to do to adjust and process things in a very healthy way.

This is a good place to be, because we get to analyze not what we could have done better, because the past is gone, we can't get that back. Rather, we analyze what we can do in the now and in the future. It also makes us take a step back and reflect in our own hearts. I knew that If I was going to live a life of recovery, I have to be brand new inside my heart. No more bitterness anger, rage, or hate. This is where God's word helped me search my heart, spirit and mind.

More so, reflection was also a time of asking myself, "Where do I go in my life" or "What do I want to do now?" Should I go back to school? What profession should I pursue? At one moment, I wanted to enlist in the military, but sadly, with all my tattoos, no branch would take me. I knew once I started to clean up my life that I wanted to help people, I just didn't know how or where to begin. Maybe Christian Counseling? Maybe I could help in my church? The worst feeling in the world for me was when I needed help in my addiction and I called so many detox centers and no one would take me unless I had money to put down. I wanted to share my struggles but no one to talk to.

However, the time I spent alone allowed me to reflect on what I wanted my life to be and who I could help. I also reflected on "Would I marry? Would I have more kids? What would I be doing when I am 30 or 40?" Reflection is good!

Search deep into your heart deep

What are the things in your life that had caused you to drink and use drugs? What were you trying to numb in your life? What were you trying to forget? What were you trying to heal from? Remember, there is a ROOT to everything we go through in life. Let's find it and cut it off at the root.

The heart is a deep and sacred place for us, we only allow certain people in that area. Most of the time, we are still suffering from the hurts of life from our past that we wonder if we really are healing the right way. Then we spend our whole life shutting people out, building up walls.

When your heart begins to get exposed through reflection and searching, you start to find YOU! We all have used that term before, "I need time to find me" or "Soul Searching."

Guess what? You're in recovery and in an awkward position. It's time to start doing some soul searching. It's time to find you. It's time to ask the heart, "What's wrong? What's going on?" We have to ask ourselves how we can get to the next chapter of our lives with a searched heart, a healed heart, a strengthened heart, and a sober and clean heart.

For so long, we have allowed drugs and alcohol to become who we are. Along the line, we might have lost ourselves in that world. In and out of prison, in and out of rehab, on the streets - whatever the case may be, we lost ourselves, and we allowed that to become so written and engraved onto our hearts that we believe that this is who we will always be.

Searching is where we must pick up after the time of reflection. We all are searching for something, every single human being walking the face of this world is searching. But little did they know that it starts in their own hearts. If we are not careful, we can spend our whole lives searching and never really finding what we are looking for. Many people will die with their hearts still not fully searched. Ask yourself, "Why do I feel this way?" Then let the searching begin.

Again, I am a Christian, and I am glad Christ searched my heart when I really needed it. He showed me who I was and what I had become. The more I searched my own heart, the more things were exposed to me. And I had a lot of work to do and I am still working on those things today.

Why I was addicted? Why did I let it go on for so long? Why did I think or act in a certain way? Why was I angry? Why was I full of hate? Why? These are the questions I searched my heart for answers.

Allow that heart to be searched, friend. Go deep, go wide and don't stop till every inch and area of your heart is searched and things are exposed. Once it is empty, NOW you can start filling it with good things and with the new you. You might want to get a journal for this thought. I know it's a lot to process and I know your wheels are turning in your head. It's okay, I get it. One thing at time, one thought at a time, one search at a time. To this day, Christ has my heart and He continues to search it daily and exposes those things which I must work on.

Once you have had a time of reflection and thoroughly searched your heart, now you:

You find.........

You find you. You find your purpose. You find your life and what it was truly meant be. It was amazing to see how clear things became in my life once I began to be clean and sober.

It was like I had a direction, and I was focused for once. This was when I began to explore the possibilities for my life. This is when I started to see that my past and my addiction is not who it says I am. The trials and mistakes in life were not going to define my life. There was more for me, more for my life, and I wanted to explore that. I was the "God" of my life for so long and it got me in trouble. Now I just wanted to be used by God in whatever way that looked like.

In this season in your life, my prayer and hope is that you find you. Reflect, search and find what you were made to be. Find your purpose, find why you were truly created. We were not created to make a mess out of our lives, we were created for a specific purpose and for something great. You have to truly believe that! You have to truly embrace it! Once you find you, once you find that purpose in life, nothing is going to get in the way of your recovery, nothing is going to make you want to go back to your old life. Because you see your new life, and you see the new you, and your now newfound purpose. I am proud of you, friend! Keep going.

Much love,
Anthony Torres

"It starts with our decisions right now in our lives. It starts with us creating a DIFFERENT family line to break this generational curse"

LETTER 49

THOUGHTS ABOUT
'GENERATIONAL CURSE'

My mom once told me a story about my great grandfather who was shot in a bar. She also shared with me how my great grandmother spent most of her time sitting at a barstool, drinking her life away. Her mom had issues with alcoholism, as well as my own mother who would later sober up.

Then you look at my dad's side, where drinking is also common. I am not sure how far this goes back as I am not aware of any stories. But with my family's history of alcoholism, it's safe to say that this is something that has been passed down from generation to generation. And the truth is we accept this in our family, for our kids and grandkids and generations to come. And I sit here and wonder: Why are things going on like this? Are we not ready to face reality? Or are we okay with history repeating itself?

Back in the day, Tuesday nights were boxing fight nights on ESPN. And my kids knew that I was going to be sitting on my couch drinking Corona. And I wouldn't drink for comfort, I would drink to get drunk, drink to get sick. I remember always sending Bella or Iliana to get me another beer, and to throw away my bottles when I was done.

I was creating an environment for my kids to one day be drinkers and I didn't even know it or see it. And I know some people reading this letter will probably say "Well, I can control my drinking at home, why can't I have a beer?" Okay, I agree with you on this. But just because you can control your drinking doesn't mean your kids can when they grow up. The history of our family line of alcoholism is repeating itself and we don't even know it. We have to break that generational curse that has been plaguing our family for years. Some families are dying from liver problems, some with multiple DWI's, some with broken marriages, some lose their loved ones in prison or death, and some have been torn apart - all from one thing: drinking.

I knew from the way my life was going in my addictions that it was more likely my kids would follow in my footsteps. It was more likely that history would repeat itself for my family, for my grandkids. But it's just not with drinking, our family has a history of being in and out of prison. We see this happening a lot more in so many families. We see dad or mom spending hard time in prison and now waiting for their kids to join them.

But hear me out on this thought, we can CHANGE this! We really can. Instead of writing letters to a parole board, we can receive letters from a college. Instead of moving in and out of prison, we can be in and out of college classes to start a career. Instead of spending nights at the bar getting drunk, we can spend nights writing a book or spend nights planning a project that will change lives. Instead of shooting up dope in our arms with a needle, we are now trying to find veins for someone else because we are a nurse.

Listen to me when I say this, you can change your life, not just yours alone, but the projection of your family history as well.

And it starts with you. It starts with our decisions right now in our lives. It starts with us creating a DIFFERENT family line to break this generational curse.

I am the first pastor in my family. Think about this for a minute. I am the first to ever lead a church and to ever write a book in my family. The first to travel to third world countries. I have been to India twice and will be going to Africa in October for mission's work. My daughter who once cried for her dad to come home, now cries out to God and worships Him who restored her family, and she sings and leads worship at our church. To experience this on Sundays is amazing to a father. My other daughter helps me run "Calcutta Mercy Café" that sponsors many children's education in India. My wife now leads women into a relationship with God. Hopefully, my son will one day serve this church in whatever role God sees fit. This is all new to us, this is what our family was created to do in the beginning. But my addiction blinded us all those years, and it derailed us for so long. But for once in our lives, we are where God needs us to be and we get to do it together. We are not a perfect family, we are just called and willing to be used by God.

My grandkids for once will experience a different life, a different way of living without addiction. My kids have seen what drinking can do to our lives, what it can do to our body. My hope as a father is that they CHOOSE not to open the doors that I did, they choose a different life than what I created in the beginning for them. And I pray as they grow up, that they continue this journey with God. Because the future of our family depends on it, from generation to generation.

And right now, you have a choice to make. Will you continue in your addiction and never break this generational curse? Will you keep on this cycle that has been passed down from your family for years? Or will you change this cycle of destruction for the future of your family and generations to come.

I am not saying it's easy, there were many times that I wanted to give up. There many times, even while serving in the church, that I wanted to do something else. Many nights sitting down looking out the window while it rained and thought "I am not sure if I can really do this." But I didn't quit, I had to stay in it and try to make a change somehow. Because I knew it was not just about me. I knew it was about my family and generations to come. And at least I wanted to do my part to change this.

Today I am praying for you that whatever generational curse you have been dealing with in your family, today is the day it's broken. Today is the day that your last name is removed from failure, destruction, depression, anxiety and all other emotional issues you are facing. Your name is now attached to value and purpose. It's attached to peace and joy for your heart. The time is now, friend. And you can do this, it doesn't matter how bad things are or how far you have gone. You have it in you to change this for your family. My prayer is that God will give you the strength to do this.

Much Love
Anthony Torres

"Scars are meant to be healed, not

meant to be reopened"

LETTER 50

THOUGHTS ABOUT
'SCARS'

I think everyone in the world has scars somewhere on their body, some are caused by us. Maybe by accidentally cutting our finger with a knife while cutting fruits or falling down scraping our knees while playing outside. I have one scar on my right finger. I was stabbed there during a fight when I was younger. Every time I see it or don't feel it (it's numb in that area), I remember the doctor saying "Any closer to this area, you would have lost your finger."

Scars are meant for one purpose; to remind us what happened or what we have been through. Many people in the world don't have just physical scars, but internal ones as well from their past. A person that is a cutter has full evidence of these scars. They know the feeling when they cut, when they release that pain, when that blood begins to come off that open wound as tears begin to roll down their face, and they know whatever emotion they are dealing with in that moment is going to be released. Now that past pain is on their body with scars, but they don't have to relive it. It's just a reminder! It has healed in their lives.

And this is what scars are. You don't have to relive any more moments again. Scars are meant to be healed, not meant to be reopened. Scars from your past, the hurts, and the pain have healed. And if they haven't, I hope they do one day, because remember I said it's hard to have a life of recovery if we keep on living the past.

As you read this book, you begin to think about a lot of scars that have healed in your life or things that need to heal to become scars. The purpose of this quick thought is this, don't apologize for those scars, don't hide your cut arms or legs, don't hide your broken heart. Don't hide what you have been through, never be ashamed. You're healed! You're restored! Let's walk worthy of that. I wear mine daily, that is why I poured my soul into this book. Look at your scars today and be thankful you have another chance in life, be thankful it's another day to be better in your recovery. Another day you can walk around saying "I am really doing this" and "I will be okay." I have scars that healed, and they remind me that new ones will heal as well. Remember, scars are meant to be healed, not meant to be reopened."

Much love,
Anthony Torres

"What are you going to do with your second chance? We don't get many of these moments back"

LETTER 51

FINAL THOUGHT ON
'HOW HIGH CAN YOU REACH?'

I'm sure right now after reading this book you're thinking, *how will things be for me in 2-5 years from now? Can I continue this journey clean and sober? Can I really do and work on the things that Anthony is talking about?* I know you have had a flood of emotions while reading this book.

In one thought, I talked about setting goals for yourself, setting yourself up to win, not to fail. Putting yourself in that position to overcome. You see, we have to ask ourselves that, where are we positioning ourselves?

You remember that board game "Battleship"? The ships are in the sea that we positioned. And depending on where we're at on that board with our ships, it could be a hit or a miss for our opponent. But remember we couldn't move our ships once they were set in place. We just had to make sure we made the right move before our opponents made theirs. If not, our battleships would sink and we would lose.

If you're still hanging around the same friends, hanging around the same environment, still in toxic relationships, same thinking, same old habits, you are putting yourself in a position to lose.

You have to make some drastic changes in your life to continue your journey of being sober and clean. Not just one month, but many months and many years of staying clean and sober. The important lesson you need to learn from this thought is: Always guard your heart and mind in recovery. Don't think because it's been years and years that you can't have a normal, good life. You have to keep the train moving every day.

But what if, just what if, one day people come to church to hear what God has put in my heart for them one Sunday, but I am not there. As they walk into church, all they can hear is people upset or even crying as they hug my family. And in the midst of the weeping, everyone is wondering what is going on.

Sasha walks up to the stage, with tears flowing in her eyes, she addresses the church as it's so quiet you can hear a pin drop, you can hear the sniffling of people. She says "Anthony did not come home the other night; from what I was told, he was back on drugs and started drinking again. At this point, we don't know where he is at, and we have lost all communication with him. I ask you to pray for him as he seems to have lost his way again." The ministry that God allowed me to have at this point would be OVER! My family's life once again would be shattered, and I would find myself in my mess again. And this Scripture comes to my mind.

Proverbs 26:11 As a dog returns to its vomit, so a fool repeats his foolishness

Or maybe you're reading this book and decided to write me. But you never received a letter back because I went back to my old ways. My credibility in writing this book is gone, and I spent all those late nights writing for nothing.

I'm sure no one saw it coming, and I'm sure I probably didn't either. Again, we cannot say because we have been clean and sober for so many months or years that we can't go back to our old ways, this is why you can't let your foot off the pedal.

Now remember what I said, I am not here to force my beliefs on you. I am sharing with you what I have to do DAILY to keep my spirit right, to keep it strong so I don't go back. To help me with those temptations that we all have daily. I'm sure people call me a Holy Roller and all kinds of other names, but this Holy Roller is trying to stay in it, this Holy Roller is trying to stay clean and sober, this Holy Roller is trying to live and not die anymore, and if it means serving Jesus all the days of my life, so be it. I have to put things in order in my personal life to guard my heart, to guard my sobriety. And guess what, friend, so do you.

I really want to challenge you with this question? What are you going to do with your second chance? We don't get many of these moments back. We just don't! I truly believe that you're not reading this book just by accident. I believe it's for a reason. I don't want you to get to the end of this book and say "That was a good read" but then don't do any reflection in your life and begin to change things. In my heart, this whole book is about reflection and change.

The other day, I was driving on a highway from Las Cruces, Nm to El Paso, Tx. It's a known highway called I-10 here in this area. I haven't been on that highway in a very long time. But I noticed there were more memorial sites on the side of the highway with crosses. And I began to think, I should have had mine on here. Because there were many nights I drove back from El Paso on my motorcycle, drunk and high. Even many nights not even knowing how I got home. I should have died on that highway. I should have died in my home. I should have died in my garage. There are times I look back and think, "How did I survive all those nights, all those dark and painful times?"

And the truth is, I don't know. I don't know how some of us make it out alive and some don't. But I got my second chance and I want to make the best of it. And I want you to make the best of it too, friend. Before I end this book and wrap up this final thought, I want to encourage you to dream of the possibilities in your life. I want you to dream even in the midst of the unknown.

I dreamed that one day I would have a family. I dreamed that one day I wouldn't wake up with hangovers anymore. I dreamed that one day my suicidal thoughts would not be so intense. I dreamed that one day I wouldn't give in to my demons of drugs. I dreamed one day that I could say, "I hit my year of being clean and sober." I dreamed that one day I would have a steady job. I dreamed one day I would finish school or at least finish something in my life. I dreamed that one day I would somehow make a difference by helping people in a place that I once was. I dreamed that one day I would look myself in the mirror and say, "You're doing it! And you're finally doing something with your life."

Fast forward to 2021, and not only did I dream, I achieved. And I saw God not only rebuild, but also restored my life. It was not easy. I had to completely give everything to Christ. All my past, all my pain, my broken heart, my broken family — everything in my life is now HIS!

Even to this day, I am still picking up the pieces to my past. It's been a journey, but even in my 40s, I am still dreaming. I am reaching for more in whatever that looks like.

Somewhere in our recovery, we think, "I have arrived." No, friend, we never arrive. We need to be reaching for more. Reaching for those dreams that are in our hearts to become a reality.

You have seen so much darkness in your life, strive for light. You have seen so much pain, you need to see healing.

You have seen so much brokenness, see being put back together. You have seen so much addiction to the point that
when they draw blood from your veins, they can't find any.
You need to experience freedom!

If you have a broken education, a dream for a degree.
Maybe you have seen so much prison walls, dream of walls in
your newly purchased home. You have seen so much un-
healthy relationships, dream for forgiving ones. You have to
have dreams. What are they? Write them down. I hear people
say, "When we think of it, it's just that, a dream. But when we
write it down, it now becomes a goal we want to achieve."
Even 11 years into this, I am still dreaming and writing down
the things I want to achieve. I want MORE of whatever God
wants for my life.

Think about this for a second, we were so sold out for our
addiction. We didn't care who we hurt, what we did, or where
we ended up. We needed MORE and wanted more of that
high. More of that addiction, one more drink, one more high.
We were SOLD OUT for it. Why not be sold out in your recovery, be sold out for your purpose in this life, in your calling, in
your gift.

Dream you can have a better life. Dream for your marriage
(if you're married). Dream for your kids. The sky is the limit
for you, friend. Don't limit God in your life, dream with a purpose.

I don't want you to have "Brick wall thinking." You're saying "What is that?" This is what it is: You've been doing drugs
for so long, you've been in and out of jail for so long. You've
had a messed life for a very long time. All you see is that brick
wall in front of you. You dream for a little bit in your life, then
you hit that wall AGAIN, then you start to say "Maybe this is
just my life. Maybe this is my destiny."

Wrong thinking! That is a lie straight from the devil himself. You have to see over that wall that there are blessings and purpose NO MATTER HOW MANY times you hit that wall. That wall is meant to keep you stuck in your wrong thinking of "This is all that life has to offer me."

So, you have to get over that "brick wall thinking." You're not screwed up, you're not trash.

Before I wrap it up, I want to say "Thank you" for taking the time to read this book. Thank you for letting me share my struggles with you, my family with you. It's been a long journey writing this book, putting these thoughts to paper, as tears fell on my keyboard. I have had many late nights thinking *how did I ever get through those times*. My wife says I probably should have started counseling before I started this book. Because I gave it everything that I had. I poured myself into this book to the point of shutting down some days.

I had many late nights writing and digging into my old life so that one day I could help someone with their new one. Many nights, my anxieties got so bad while thinking. I didn't sleep well, but I was able to write. I write not to make me known, I write so you can see you don't have to stay stuck.

I had to open a lot of old wounds that healed. I had to relive some areas in my life that I have forgotten about. But I knew I needed to do this to help someone out there. Someone that needed a word of encouragement, a word of truth. A book that was going to be so real, it would touch the core of your soul and heart. That when you are done reading it, you won't feel like you are the only one dealing with things emotionally and spiritually. Christian or not, we all need HOPE in this life. We need hope in our addictions. Mine is Jesus, every minute, every day.

My hope and desire is that this book helps you somehow, whether you believe in God or not. My hope is that after you're done with this book, you can say "If this guy can do it, so can I. If God can use his past to help others, He can use mine too."

I am not perfect! I never will be. I am just a guy that wanted to share his story with the world. That as long as you're breathing and alive today, no matter how bad your life looks, there is always HOPE. That in that darkness, there is light. In that pain, there is healing. These are "Letters to my people" because you will always be a part of me, no matter where you are at in the world. Recovering addicts have a special bond, I believe. We share the same struggle, we have a bond like no other. We get each other. This is it!

It's the ending, and now you have what you need to get on a road of being sober and clean and to continue to stay on this road. You will always be in my heart, and always in my prayers. Your life is not over yet. Get busy, keep dreaming and keep believing. If this book helped you, pass it on to another person that needs it. Goodbye, God bless, and take care of yourself. You were created for great things.

Much love forever,
Anthony Torres

ABOUT THE AUTHOR

Anthony Torres was born in Altus, Ok. He grew up in Las Cruces, Nm. And now resides in Alamogordo, Nm with his wife Sasha Torres. He is the father of 4 wonderful kids. He is the Pastor of MountainVIEW Church, a Church that is outreach driven to REACH1 in its community, he also the founder of "New Life Recovery" His heart is to see people set free from Addictions. Connect with him on Social media.

Facebook@reach1forHOPE
Instagram@recovered_addict09

Anthony and his wife Sasha have been the Pastors of MountainVIEW Church since 2015 in Alamogordo,Nm. They started off with only 20 people in attendance. Today 2021, they have over 300 people that call MountainVIEW Church home. And still growing today. Their hearts are to minister Jesus to broken people, speaking about the love, forgiveness, and rebuilt lives that Jesus offers.

Anthony loves street ministry, and creating a movement to reach1 on the streets with outreach in the city monthly.

Sasha is the overseer of womens ministry and Calcutta Mercy Café that sponsors children monthly in Calcutta, India for an education. If you like to write Anthony you can send letters to MountainVIEW Church, 1300 Cuba ave Alamogordo,NM 88310: Attention Anthony Torres. Or you can email him at Anthony@mvagalamo.com. Check out the churches website at www.mvcalamo.com

If you would like Anthony to speak at any event or come speak in the prisons email him at: Anthony@mvagalamo.com

Made in the USA
Coppell, TX
30 January 2024

28407319R00197